Praise for
You're Invited

"Bold, crisp, refreshing and very practical! Those are just some of the words that come to my mind after reading Joe Saladino's new book. From the first page he had my undivided attention. I don't ever recall an author starting out with such an attention-grabbing confession. As a lifelong pastor and pastor's son, I have read a lot of books and listened to a lot of sermons over the past sixty years. My mantra has been, "Either tell me something NEW or at least make what I have already heard all of my life INTERESTING!" Well, Joe has done both! For anyone who has struggled to live a life of victory, Joe has provided some of the most practical tools I have ever seen based upon legal principles that are irrefutable. This book will be a training manual that is referenced again and again."

—Jere Webb, Real Estate Broker,
Former Pastor/Evangelist jw@JereWebb.com

"Joe Saladino has uncovered an area of spiritual warfare that gets little attention, but it dramatically empowers our journey with God! I have seen the principles taught in his book applied with stunning results! It is well worth your time to find out why they work."

—Troy Haagenson, Pastor
PastorTroy@Cloverdale.org

"Many will face heartbreak and hopelessness in their relationship; however, both happiness and forgiveness are a choice. There can be trust, love, and intimacy in the wake of a betrayal. This book methodically reveals the necessary tools for all couples to walk hand-in-hand with the Lord on their journey to spiritual and emotional healing."

—Zlata Plumlee, J.D. Candidate 2020,
Lewis & Clark Law School, zgolberg@lclark.edu

"Joe Saladino has managed to put down in book form how the gospel births the power of healing victory in the lives of believers. He explains the method he uses with great success in his counseling ministry. This is a refreshingly new approach to victory over particularly oppressive sins that tend to break the spirit of believers in their attempt to gain freedom from them. His relating of how this new approach has been effective in the lives of his clients will thrill you to try it in your own lives. I heartily recommend you read the powerful account of his successful experience in his ministry of healing."

—Jerry Willis, Retired Pastor

"Are you bewildered by unresolved personal and relational problems that persist despite your good intentions and efforts to do better? Years of frustration and pain lead us to walk away from relationships, abandon dreams, and give up faith. What's the point when nothing works? In this book, Joe Saladino shares what he learned on his quest to help himself, his loved ones, and others. In our increasingly post-modern world of relativistic thinking, we have lost sight of the power of solid stable truth. Whether you've struggled five months or fifty-five years in a hopeless situation, Joe's practical instructions of how anyone anywhere can get life-long lasting relief from the despair of defeat are priceless. Our modern monster of inner stress and turmoil can be tamed by the plain truth. The results are truly astounding."

—Sara Abatiell, Designer Analyst

YOU'RE INVITED

to discover
a predictable path to
peace, joy, and freedom

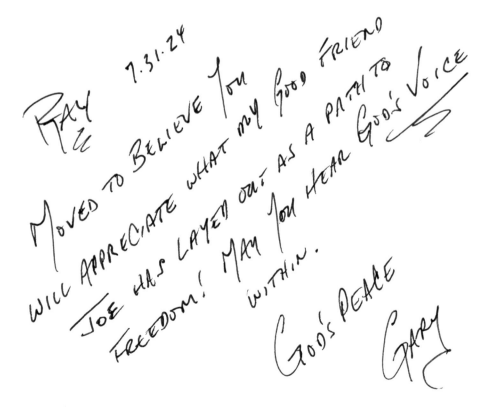

RAY
7.31.24

Moved to Believe You
will Appreciate what my good friend
Joe has layed out as a path to
freedom! May you hear God's Voice
within.

God's Peace

Gary

Joseph Oquendo Saladino

Table of Contents

To Cissa, my wife of forty-nine years,
who loves me with an uncommon and Godly love.

FOREWORD:
A Way Out of Bondage into a
Dynamic Christian Life

John A. Eidsmoe,

Chaplain (Colonel), Mississippi State Guard, Retired Air Force Judge Advocate;
Senior Counsel, Foundation for Moral Law; Professor of Constitutional Law, Oak
Brook College of Law; Pastor, Association of Free Lutheran Congregations

How many Christians say they want their spiritual lives transformed? A conservative estimate would be about ninety-nine percent.

No wonder, then, that the shelves of Christian bookstores are packed with books on how to become a dynamic Christian. Commonly, these books take one of two approaches:

(1) Get to work, discipline yourself, sacrifice, train, and build! The path to spiritual strength is much like bodybuilding at a spiritual gym; or

(2) Relax, surrender to the Holy Spirit, and let Him take over and do the work for you.

There is truth in both of these approaches, but each is missing something. The first gives too much credit to human effort, forgetting that spirituality, like salvation, is by grace through faith. The second ignores that God uses our efforts to build us. The Bible uses military metaphors ("I have fought a good fight," II Timothy 4:7), athletic metaphors ("Let us run the race that is now before us," Hebrews 12:1), and academic metaphors ("Study to show thyself approved before God, a workman that needeth not to be ashamed," II Timothy 2:15) for the process of spiritual growth or sanctification.

In *You're Invited*, Joseph Saladino avoids both of these pitfalls. He says we must take responsibility for our spiritual condition because that condition is the result of decisions we have made, contracts we have chosen to enter into. Drawing upon contract law, he says we are bound in sin because we have chosen to believe Satan's lies and have entered into contract with him. But under the law, contracts can be broken when induced by fraud, and Satan's contracts with us are void or voidable because we entered into them believing Satan's lies and misrepresentations.

How can you transform your spiritual life? By embracing God's Truth as revealed in Scripture and, thus renouncing Satan's lies, you are freed from bondage to him and free to follow Christ.

Likewise, following Satan's lies can lead us into hard-heartedness and bitterness. When someone has sinned against us, we believe Satan's lie that this sin is unforgivable or that the person is not really repentant. By coming to the truth, we can learn to forgive, be free from the burden of bitterness, and receive the blessing of renewed relationships.

Intensely Biblical, *You're Invited* is also intensely practical. Born amidst the author's own spiritual struggles, Saladino details for us step-by-step how to recognize Satan's lies, how to replace them with the Truth of God's Word, how to step out from under the bondage of Satan's falsely-induced contracts, and how to step forward into new spiritual life with Christ.

So, are you among the ninety-nine percent who believe their spiritual lives could stand some improvement? Are you among those who want spiritual transformation but aren't sure where or how to start? If so, read Joseph Saladino's book.

That's my invitation to you. *You're Invited!*

Full Disclosure

As you read *You're Invited*, you will understand how passionate I am about the law. Many of the principles in this book came together for me while in prison. After battling with the government for several years, I was convicted for defrauding the United States. The two-thousand-member organization I started sued the government over two hundred times demanding answers to questions the government could but would not answer. In each interaction with the government, I followed the law to the letter—and every 1040 return we filed included a two-page affidavit which explained exactly what our claim was. At the local and appellate court levels, the government consistently refused to respond to my briefs with any rigorous review and ruling by the judges. When I finally took my case to the United States Supreme Court, it was denied without comment again. Attorneys who read my Supreme Court brief[1] say that according to the rule of law I should've won my case. And while I followed the law to the letter, at the end of the day, it was of no consequence. After many battles, in 2009, I was sentenced as a felon to five years in prison.

My job is not to restore judicial integrity to the United States. For this reason, I recommend that everyone live within the system

---

1. Information of this brief can be found on the website *Supreme Court United States* using case number 06-461. The brief can be viewed online at the following link: http://h4hm.org/book-docs/SC-Case-2013-00.pdf.

as much as possible and make every effort to pursue God and His Kingdom which are eternal.

I must admit that after the dust settled, I had my moments with God. Where was the benefit in losing my case at every level? Throughout these battles, I followed what I thought was God's direction, and when I expected God to show up, He didn't. I struggled with bitterness over my expectations. During the years of my incarceration, God began to change my focus. And He healed my heart. Being in prison was the perfect place to take up my new assignment: to test and develop the *freedom protocol* by which the heart can experience the abundant life of peace and joy.

Contained herein are biblical principles of the freedom protocol. I have effectively used these principles in my personal life and counseling ministry for many years. They are not theory. When implemented, they produce powerful, predictable results.

The freedom protocol helped me see that victory over the power of sin is only possible when we understand God's provisions for us. Our Heavenly Father has supreme authority to which He has given us access. Once authority in the context of God's law is understood, believed, and integrated into one's life, God-sized things begin to happen. One begins to believe that victory over sin and the abundant life Jesus promised is possible today, not just a distant hope.

If you approach this protocol as just a concept to think about, little will change in your life. If you apply its principles, you can expect God to move in your heart and life. He will meet you where you are and take the weight and failure of your sin upon Himself. He will deliver you from the things holding you down and holding you back. He will become the powerful and engaging God your heart always desired Him to be. Then you can confidently expect your life to change.

PART 1:

Laying the Groundwork

Chapter One:

RSVP

victory, noun[2]

vic·to·ry | \ ˈvik-t(ə-)rē

1: the overcoming of an enemy or antagonist

2: achievement of mastery or success in a struggle or endeavor against odds or difficulties

What if by a change in our thinking, we could have more victory in our lives? Paul the apostle said, "I pray . . . that you may know the hope to which He has called you" (Eph. 1:18). According to the gospel, ALL are invited to know this hope. God has intentionally made Himself approachable, understandable, and reasonable, especially as we make the effort to *know* His ways. He has not hidden Himself from us but rather, we've at times hidden from Him or have created our own definition of who He is, maybe even unknowingly. In believing a false narrative about God, we will find ourselves drifting away from Him, feeling the weight of failures over sin, and white-knuckling[3] our way through life and relationships.

During the years I have been counseling, I have discovered similarities in daily life struggles that have caused a major shift in my

---

2. Merriam Webster, s.v. "victory," https://www.merriam-webster.com/dictionary/victory

3. The words white-knuckle are often used to describe a situation where something is leading to intense nervousness or fear. A good example would be a scary rollercoaster; people just grab onto the handrails as tight as they can and wait for it to be over.

thinking. I began to view these struggles through a deeper under-standing of God's justice and mercy. At every juncture, underlying and foundational principles of who God is and how He interacts with us had proven simple to understand and implement—and more important, effective. I watched people quickly find freedom in daily life.

Does that sound like a freedom to be desired? What if you could be less harassed[4] and tormented by the enemy? Imagine being free of addictions or the enemy's relentless temptations. What if the enemy could be put in his place so that you could rule over sin in your life and finally get some blood back in your white knuckles? Well, if you are up to the challenge, fasten your seat belts—by accepting this invitation, life is about to change for the better.

God's Word invites us to discover how His justice and mercy relate to our struggles with temptation and sin. This invitation includes practical teaching on how to experience God to the full-est and how His ways empower us to be overcomers of sin and struggles, such as depression, anxiety, fear, bitterness, and other life-controlling problems. In the coming chapters, I discuss what the Bible says and shows about temptation and sin, how God relates to both mankind and the enemy of our souls regarding temptation and sin, and that His plan of redemption and character of justice has provided a way for us to be free from the strongholds of sin. You'll read about principles of law and how they help us relate to God. I also discuss the biblical definition of sin and give practical examples from people who have experienced freedom by embracing and implementing these biblical principles. Below is a brief descrip-tion of the following chapters in this book:

---

4. The term "harassed" as used here means temptations without any parameters or limita-tions. The enemy comes and goes into our lives at will and without any limitations.

PART ONE: LAYING THE GROUNDWORK

- **Freedom Protocol** *is a process rooted in biblical principles and principles of law that effectively positions us to rule over sin by accessing God's authority over the enemy.*

- **Temptation and the Rules of Engagement** *shows how God interfaces with us, and how Satan interfaces with God and us. There appear to be rules from biblical examples that provide us predictability when it comes to dealing with temptation, sin, and the enemy of our souls.*

- **Truth and Lies** *identifies how the truths and lies we have believed play a crucial part in successfully ruling over sin by exercising the freedom protocol.*

- **Contracts** *puts wheels on the rules of engagement and shows how we make contracts with the enemy by what we choose to believe—his lies or God's truth.*

- **Ruling Over Sin** *gives an understanding of what God expects from us. If we don't know what God expects, then we are adrift like a ship without a rudder.*

- **What Is Sin?** *defines sin from a biblical perspective.*

- **Only by God's Authority** *draws the line between the white-knuckle experience and the abundant life and shows that God reigns supreme, having all authority.*

- **Identifying Lies** *gives a list of indicators intended to help you identify the lies of the enemy and the truth of God.*

- **Forgiveness** *shows how to identify people in our lives whom we need to forgive, leading us to resolve bitterness at a deeper level.*

PART TWO: PRACTICAL APPLICATIONS

- **Let's Get Started** *is a step-by-step guide to using the freedom protocol.*

- **Pride and Humility** *exemplifies how truths and lies, as they are presented and revealed to us by the Holy Spirit, affect pride and humility in our lives.*

- **Hardships and Trials** *looks at the reality of challenges we experience as we seek to know God on a deeper level and to rule over sin in our lives.*

- **Vigilance and Perseverance** *talks about how to maintain our freedom over the long haul.*

- **Is Jesus Necessary?** *takes a hard look at the role Jesus plays in our search for the truth that will set us free.*

Each of these chapters is a vital part of understanding how God's character calls us to rule over sin. *You're Invited* can be used as a manual to be read and referred to often, as you experience more and more victory over the power of sin.

If you are tired of white-knuckling your way through life,
If you believe that living for God is too difficult or impossible,
If you feel you are in a hopeless bondage to sin,
If you have prayed, fought, and negotiated to be free without relief,
If you have spent years living a defeated life,
If the pressures of life have pushed you to the point of despair,
If your life is filled with chaos, confusion, or conflict on any level,
If your marriage is in trouble and hope is a distant memory,
This book is for you.

Chapter Two:

Freedom Protocol

In this chapter, I introduce you to the freedom protocol. It is very likely you're familiar with its principles or have seen them before in some form. Don't be alarmed at the word protocol; it's just an easy way to say *steps that help us experience God's character and love—steps that give us a way to work out His invitation to rule over sin and enjoy the abundant life.* This protocol is meant to be a simple framework to use in daily life, thereby creating a biblical framework that leads to freedom. The name freedom protocol is not in the Bible, but its principles are seen throughout as I will show in the coming chapters.

Books written about victory over the power of sin generally talk about having *more* of something in our lives, such as prayer, Bible study, the Holy Spirit, willpower, discipline, or obedience. While we should have these in our lives in increasing amounts, power over sin is not just about having more of something, but about the authority of God. We do not possess this authority. It resides in God and is exercised *by us* through the One who saves us. Most encouraging, as children of God we all have equal rights and access to this authority.

God has not abandoned us as we battle against the enemy and his temptations but has given us the Holy Spirit who leads us to all truth. The freedom protocol deals with the plan, or remedies, God has provided to free us from sins that keep us stuck or habitually out of fellowship with Him. When we exercise the freedom protocol, God backs it up with His power and authority, and we experience immediate results and relief. Understanding God's remedies to deal with sin will help us access those remedies and obtain freedom and the abundant life God invites us to and promises us in His Word.

THE FREEDOM PROTOCOL

The following protocol shows a biblical process that when exercised gives us victory over the power of sin:

1. Identify the lie(s) of the enemy you believed.[5]

2. Identify the respective truth(s) as revealed by God.

3. Repent (change your mind) from believing the lies to believing the truth.

4. Renounce the lies and embrace the truth as revealed by God.

5. Take back the access you granted to the enemy by believing his lies.

6. Return that access back to God and ask Him to protect you from the enemy.

Let's define a few words for their intended purposes, in order to help you navigate your way through this book:

- **protocol**—an accepted way of conducting oneself in a given situation; a pre-established method of carrying out a task and especially a scientific or medical task.[6] In the context of the freedom protocol: rules, or steps, by which we interact with the enemy and with God. Knowing these rules of engagement will help deliver you from the power of sin.

---

5. One can start with identifying the lie(s) or the truth(s)—but before moving on to step three, it is best to identify both the lie(s) and the truth(s).

6. *Merriam-Webster*, s.v. "protocol." https://www.merriam-webster.com/thesaurus/protocol.

- **remedy**—a method of legally solving a problem or disagreement.[7] In the context of the freedom protocol: God-given remedies intended to rescue us from the power of sin. When we exercise these remedies, we get predictable relief from an undesirable circumstance.

- **salvation**—the act of saving; preservation from destruction, danger, or great calamity.[8] In our context, this is the overall plan devised by God to weed out and destroy sin, and to restore us to Himself.

- **repentance**—to change one's mind.[9]

- **renounce**— to give up, refuse, or resign usually by formal declaration.[10] In our context, we release our claim and belief in the enemy's lies.

Implementing the freedom protocol changes the way you converse with God. While prayer, Bible study, fasting, meditation, fellowship, and the Holy Spirit are vital to the victorious life, I find it is the *role* these play in the Christian life that is often misunderstood. This misunderstanding creates confusion and leads many to despair because they never really know when they have enough of "it" in their lives. For example, prayer is one way to communicate with our Creator. The question is, "What do we talk to God about?" If you are in battle and huddled in a foxhole with a walkie-talkie in your hand, connected directly to the commanding General, what would be the subject of your conversation? At that moment, would you ask

---

7. *Cambridge Dictionary*, s.v. "Remedy." https://dictionary.cambridge.org/us/dictionary/english/remedy

8. *Webster's Dictionary 1828 Online*, s.v. "Salvation." http://webstersdictionary1828.com/Dictionary/salvation

9. *Merriam-Webster*, s.v. "Repent." https://www.merriam-webster.com/dictionary/repent

10. *Merriam-Webster*, s.v. "Renounce." https://www.merriam-webster.com/dictionary/renounce

the General to bring you a sandwich or ask why your buddy has new boots and you do not? Your communication would be about the battle, how to fight effectively, or about praise and gratitude to the General for the support he gave you. God invites us to talk to Him about our trials, financial issues, important decisions, people who are wounding us, etc. As you go through the process of implementing the freedom protocol, you will discover your conversations with God become specific as you identify the enemy's lies and ask God to lawfully take action against the enemy on your behalf.

How do we identify all the lies we have been led to believe? Simple: God's Word as it stands—the gold standard of truth. The Bible is one way in which God reveals the truth that can set us free. It's a vital treasure-house of God's thoughts written to show us what is false and what is true. All of us have been overwhelmed with lies of the enemy over the years and, worse, we actually believe them to be true. The Bible is a source of living truths, waiting to be discovered. When those truths are believed and embraced, they will have a profound, long-lasting impact on your life.

The Holy Spirit is a vital source of truth, but His role in our lives is often misunderstood. Generally, when the Holy Spirit is discussed, it is in the context of getting more power—the focus on power as strength, not power as authority. However, the Holy Spirit's job is very simple and expressed clearly by Jesus:

> *"But when he, the Spirit of truth, comes, he will guide you into all the truth. He will not speak on his own; he will speak only what he hears, and he will tell you what is yet to come" (John 16:13 New International Version, NIV[11]).*

The Christian life is not about the Holy Spirit turning a one-hundred-pound weakling into a "Popeye" or muscle-man. The

---

11. Unless otherwise indicated, all Bible references are from the New International Version (NIV).

Spirit's role is to bring us the truth. The prophet Isaiah tells us that He is a guide to help us navigate the uncharted waters of life:

Whether you turn to the right or to the left, your ears will hear a voice behind you, saying, "This is the way; walk in it" (Isa. 30:21).

In these verses, we see the Holy Spirit's job is to lead us to the truth so we can experience the freedom God longs for us to have. This is not done by strength power but by authority power—God's authority, rooted in the principles of law that were designed by God at the beginning of time. Once authority in the context of God's law and His justice is understood, believed, embraced, and implemented, your life starts to change. You will begin to believe that the abundant life is possible today. Right now.

God calls us to test Him, to reason with Him.

Taste and see that the LORD is good; blessed is the one who takes refuge in him (Ps. 34:8).

"Come now, and let us reason together," saith the Lord (Isa. 1:18a King James Version, KJV).

"Test me in this," says the LORD Almighty, "and see if I will not throw open the floodgates of heaven and pour out so much blessing that there will not be room enough to store it" (Mal. 3:10[12]).

As we actively use the freedom protocol, we should expect God to move in our hearts and lives. We should expect to experience victory over sin. We will discover that He meets us where we are but never leaves us where we are.

---

12. The context of this verse is returning a tithe of our income to God. Regardless of the context, it is still true that God invites us to prove Him, reason with Him, and taste and see that He is who He says He is.

Chapter Three:

Temptation and the Rules of Engagement

In this chapter we begin to specifically answer why God's protocol for dealing with sin is so powerfully effective. Keeping in mind God has all power and authority, there are rules of engagement evidenced in scripture that exemplify how God interfaces with His creation. These rules show why the freedom protocol works, why it gives us an edge over the enemy, and how God prepared a way for us to overcome sin. We are able to see more clearly why we are harassed by the enemy or why we're struggling with temptation.

Every society has laws that regulate how its members function together. Companies have established ways of doing business that are organized with written policies and procedures. Families also have specific ways in which they interact among themselves and with others; these "laws" are often unwritten, but they are generally understood by each member of that society. For example, when our children were young, we often said, "Other families might do that but that is not how the Saladino's behave." Even lawless individuals in prison establish their own rules to govern their daily lives while incarcerated. Inmates have both spoken and unspoken rules governing how they interact with each other, even how they conduct themselves during mealtime. The military has specific laws that govern the manner in which they protect our country. These types of written and unwritten laws, established to govern companies, families, prisoners, militaries, and many other societal groups, may be referred to as rules of engagement.

Certain rules of engagement relate to temptation and our interaction with God and the enemy. Even though the enemy and his actions may not seem to follow any discernable pattern, it is not a stretch to consider that God, the Author of law, would have established rules dictating how the enemy may approach us and interact with the world He created and is actively redeeming. Not every issue related to temptation can be addressed here, but we will analyze a few key points to help identify some rules as we deal with the enemy and his temptations. These rules of engagement are predictable, and by understanding and applying them, we can be delivered from the power of sin and temptation.

Why is it that we naturally gravitate toward law to govern us? Since we are created in God's image and He is the Author of law, is it any wonder that we have a natural bent toward order? If given the choice, few would choose to live in a chaotic, lawless society. For this reason, it appears that law is part of the security we crave, even a part of our DNA. But no one is exempt from temptation, the enemy's interactions with us.

Scripture says that we are tempted both by the enemy and by our own lusts or desires.[13] But why do some people seem to handle temptation better than others? Why is the intensity of temptation regarding any particular sin not the same for everyone? The answer is there are two individuals in the universe who can grant the enemy access to my life—God and Me. This truth shows itself in the first rule of engagement:

When God grants the enemy access to our lives, it's always with parameters.

13. See Mark 1:13, Matthew 4:1-11, and James 1:14-16.

WHEN GOD GRANTS THE ENEMY ACCESS

Below we'll look at illustrations from scripture to identify the rule that when God's the one granting the enemy access, He always sets parameters, or limitations. We'll see how God allowed the enemy to tempt Job, Peter, and Jesus but with parameters. Let's take a look.

JOB'S TEMPTATION

The Bible records an account of a righteous man named Job. Job chapter one describes a conversation between the Lord and Satan. Paraphrased, it says that Satan, the enemy, meets with God[14] along with all the sons of God, and God tells Satan to consider Job because he is a righteous man. Satan remarks that of course he's righteous because God has given[15] him everything, including protection over his entire household. Satan continues that if God were to start taking stuff away, he would curse God to His face. God says in verse twelve, "'Very well, then, everything he [Job] has is in your power, but on the man himself do not lay a finger.' Then Satan went out from the presence of the LORD."

God grants the enemy access to Job but with[16] limits on his actions, meaning God granted him permission, but it was with parameters.

---

14. Job 1:6-22

15. Job was a sinner just like us, but God regarded him as righteous because in his heart he followed and obeyed God. A sinner who is in Christ and has a heart for God is regarded as righteous by God. Let's be clear, the remedies provided by God are designed for sinners who have a great need, just like Job. It is the sinner to whom God gives access to these remedies. Jesus won for us the right to have this access. "He who has the Son has life, he who does not have the Son of God does not have life" I John 5:12.

16. Since everything God does is redemptive, we can conclude that God used this circumstance to weed out any self-righteous attitudes Job had. While he was a righteous man by doing what God had commanded him to do, it seemed, to me, he didn't grasp that he was a sinner like everyone else. Perhaps it took these drastic measures to get through to Job's heart.

After reading these verses, one might wonder if the enemy must always ask and get permission from God before he can tempt us. Does God always grant access and establish parameters for the enemy in every temptation?

In chapter two of Job, Satan is before God again under the same circumstances[17] and a similar conversation arises. God asks Satan if he has considered Job, saying that Job is a righteous man. Satan remarks that of course he's righteous because "he doesn't have any skin in the game," and that if God were to touch him, causing Job to suffer personally in his own flesh, he'd curse God to his face (Job 2:1-4). God says, "Very well, then, he is in your hands; but you must spare his life" (Job 2:6).

Again, God sets the limits. Job's story seems to indicate that this pattern of permission and parameters could be an important part of the rules of engagement regarding temptation and our interactions with God and the enemy.

PETER'S TEMPTATION

Another instance involving temptation is Jesus talking to Simon Peter and the other disciples[18] just before His crucifixion. Jesus tells Simon Peter the following:

> *"Simon, Simon, behold, Satan hath desired [demanded/asked] to have you, that he may sift you as wheat: But I have prayed for you . . ."*
> *(Luke 22:31,32 KJV; emphasis mine).* [19]

Jesus was telling Peter that he and the other disciples were going to be severely tempted but that He had prayed for them (the word

---

17. Job 2:1-10

18. Luke 22:31-32

19. The Benson Commentary on Luke 22:31-34 states that the term sift you as wheat means assault you by furious and violent temptations, or to try you to the uttermost.

"you" in the Greek is plural). It is likely that Jesus was referring to Peter's denial which was soon to take place but widened the application to include all the disciples.

In this circumstance there are no apparent parameters, but there certainly seems to be permission requested (*Satan hath desired*) and granted. Otherwise, why would Jesus need to pray for Peter? Even though there are no visible parameters suggested in this passage, it is interesting that Peter at that time was tempted only three times to deny Christ.

JESUS' TEMPTATION

Another illustration is the temptation of Jesus that followed His baptism by John the Baptist.[20] Matthew says that Jesus was "led" (other translations say "driven") by the Holy Spirit into the wilderness to be tempted.

Then Jesus was led by the Spirit into the wilderness to be tempted by the devil (Matt. 4:1).

The fact that Jesus was led by the Holy Spirit indicates that permission was granted for Jesus to be tempted. But what about parameters? While not stated directly, there appear to have been some parameters in effect:

1. For Jesus to be the perfect Lamb of God, He had to be a perfect sacrifice to take away the sin of the world. He could not be lame or have any broken bones and still be our Savior, or sacrifice.[21] One parameter may have been that the enemy could not hurt or maim Jesus, which would

---

20. Matt 3:16 – 17 4:1

21. Deuteronomy 15:21 states that for an Israelite's sacrifice to be acceptable, it must not be of a blind or lame animal—this reference is not just about physical perfection. The message God is conveying to us is that Jesus—the lamb of God who takes away the sin of the world—was without blemish morally, without sin. However, had Jesus been lame or blind

disqualify Him as the perfect sacrifice for sin,[22] similar to
God telling the enemy that he could not touch Job. This
gives us pause when we realize that the enemy took Jesus
to the top of the temple and tempted Him to cast *Himself*
down. The enemy could not hurt Jesus by pushing Him off
the temple, thereby maiming Him, but he could attempt
to persuade Jesus to cast Himself down from the temple
voluntarily. Not only would Jesus have sinned if He had
tested God, but He would likely have been disqualified as
a perfect sacrifice for sin because of broken bones from the
impact of a fall from that height.

*If an animal has a defect, is lame or blind, or has any serious
flaw, you must not sacrifice it to the LORD your God (Deut.
15:21).*

2.   Jesus was tempted only three times. When was the last time
the enemy tempted you only three times and walked away?
Compare Jesus' experience to our experiences of being end-
lessly harassed and tormented with temptation. We see the
same number of temptations with Peter. One parameter
God may have imposed on the enemy is a limitation of
three temptations. While parameters are not specifically
identified here, they are certainly consistent with the idea
of permission with parameters.

These accounts have profound implications:

---

at the time of His sacrifice for sin, it would have presented a monumental obstacle to the
Jews, further preventing them from accepting Jesus as the Messiah.

22. Not only was the sacrifice to be a perfect sacrifice (Leviticus 22:20), but the priest who
approached God could not be blemished (Numbers 8:24-25). Both the sacrifice and the
priest had to be perfect and without defect because they both represented Jesus Christ, who
stands in our place as the perfect sacrifice for sin and as a perfect priest who represents us
before the Father continually.

1. The enemy must have needed God's permission to tempt Jesus.

2. God would either grant or deny access.

3. When God does grant the enemy access, it's with parameters.

The image in figure 1 demonstrates Jesus' relationship to the enemy and his temptations.

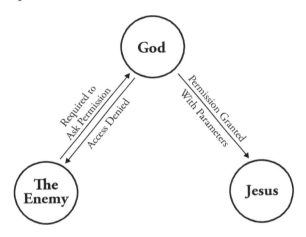

FIGURE 1. When God grants the enemy access.

Paul seems to support the idea of God granting permission with parameters when he wrote the following:

> *No temptation has overtaken you except what is common to mankind. And God is faithful; he will not <u>let</u>[23] [permission] you be tempted beyond what you can bear. But when you are tempted, he will also <u>provide a way out</u> [parameters with limitations] <u>so that you can endure it</u> (I Cor. 10:13; emphasis mine).*

These parameters God imposed upon the enemy represent the protection He provided to Job, Peter, and Jesus. And this remedy is available to us as well. Remember, at this point, since temptation

---

23. *Let* means to allow, permit, let alone.
Strong's Concordance, s.v. "1439: let." https://biblehub.com/greek/1439.htm

itself is not a sin, these examples are only about how the enemy gains access to our lives. Later, we will discuss when temptation becomes sin.

Since God has chosen to regulate the enemy's access to us, isn't God unjust to allow some to be exposed to relatively little amounts of temptation while others seem to have unbearable and unmanageable amounts of temptation? If He allows seemingly inconsistent harassment from the enemy, isn't He orchestrating some to fall into sin more often?

> For all His ways are just; a God of faithfulness and without injustice . . . (Deut. 32:4 New American Standard Bible, NASB).

Because it is God's nature to be perfectly just[24], there must be an element of these rules of engagement that we have not considered or have misunderstood, which leads to our second rule of engagement:

When *we* grant the enemy access, it is always *without* parameters—leaving us open to his harassing temptations.

Let's take a closer look.

WHEN WE GRANT THE ENEMY ACCESS

Of our own free will, all of us can grant the enemy access, or permission, apart from God's protection by simply yielding to the enemy's temptations. Relative to the access *we* grant him, the enemy is free to come and go at will; effectively, we allow him to harass us without limitations.

---

24. For further study, see the following scriptures: Isaiah 61:8, 30:18; Job 34:12; Deuteronomy 43:4; Colossians 3:25; Psalm 92:15; Micah 6:8; Psalm 37:27-39; Zechariah 7:9; Deuteronomy 16:20; Leviticus 19:15.

The Oxford English Dictionary describes harass as "subject to aggressive pressure or intimidation"; synonyms for harass are hound, torment, exasperate, worry, provoke, and bait.

We are powerless to make the enemy do anything in our own strength. Thankfully there is no evidence in scripture where God grants the enemy unlimited access, or permission, to harass us with temptation—quite the contrary, God has given us a way of escape:

No testing has overtaken you that is not common to everyone. God is faithful, and he will not let you be tested beyond your strength, but with the testing he will also provide the way out so that you may be able to endure it (I Cor. 10:13 New Revised Standard Version, NRSV).

By definition, harassment has no parameters. This type of harassing temptation without end would only involve the enemy and me. By our giving the enemy permission, we give the enemy easier access to our lives. That access can last indefinitely without relief.

The image in figure 2 demonstrates our relationship to the enemy and his temptations as a direct result of sin.[25]

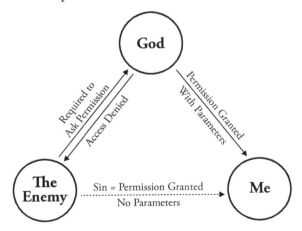

FIGURE 2. When we grant the enemy access.

25. When showing the illustration above, I am always asked why I use a dashed line between the enemy and me, and not a solid line. I use a dashed line because this relationship is not required, does not have to exist, and can be broken.

By now, we can see the frustration that can affect our lives. I have met many people who were overwhelmed by repetitive and tormenting temptation and sin; they wonder why I Corinthians 10:13 does not seem to hold true for them. This confusion is caused by a misunderstanding about who God is (His nature) and what the rules of engagement are. This confusion can lead to discouragement, depression, and despair. It appears that I Corinthians 10:13 only applies when *God grants* the enemy access to our lives, *not us*.

IS VICTORY POSSIBLE?

If what we have considered is true, then we should be able to find victory over the sin which has relentlessly harassed and tormented us. In fact, many have predictably been successful in breaking a particular bondage of sin with which they have struggled for decades by applying these insights.

JOHN, A TRAVELING SALESMAN

John spent many hours driving alone in his car and had been obsessed with pornography for over fifteen years. He went to church each week and often asked God to take away his addiction. Every time he was tempted, he resisted for a while. Sooner or later he would fall to the harassing temptations and indulge again, only to be more discouraged and depressed by his failure. By understanding temptation rules of engagement and by dealing with sin according to the freedom protocol, in a matter of a few hours, John was free and clean of his addiction for the first time. Three weeks later, John called me: "Joe, I just realized this morning—I haven't had a single pornographic thought in three weeks."

In my counseling session with John, he had discovered lies he'd been believing about pornography. He renounced those lies, embraced the truth, and asked God to take back the permission he had given to the enemy.

Let's look at how John used the freedom protocol, step by step:

1. <u>Identify the lie of the enemy you believed</u>:
   John believed the lies that pornography was okay because *he wasn't hurting anyone, he and his wife were doing it together, and it was helping his sex life.*

2. <u>Identify the respective truth as revealed through God</u>:
   For the first time, John understood the truth about pornography. He discovered that *it did not improve his relationship with his wife, it was an activity that led him to isolation, it caused him to make his wife and other women sex objects* and *to seek 'fun' without any responsibility*[26]—*it subjected him to the enemy's harassment of impure thoughts.*

3. <u>Repent (change your mind) from believing the lie to believing the truth</u>:
   John was tired of the failures in his life, but for the protocol to be effective, he had to repent (change his mind) about believing the lies, and, instead, believe and embrace God's view of pornography.

4. <u>Renounce the lie believed and instead, believe and embrace the truth as revealed by God</u>:
   Once John identified the lies and truths, and repented, he verbally renounced the identified lies and embraced the identified truths.

5. <u>Take back the access you granted to the enemy by believing his lie</u>:
   John lawfully took back, or voided, the permission he had given to the enemy, and asked God to break the enemy's strongholds in his life.

6. <u>Return that access back to God and ask Him to protect you from the enemy</u>:
   John gave the permission he had once given to the enemy back to God. He asked God to watch over his heart and protect him from the enemy's temptations.

---

26. For example, the woman in the porn video would never ask him to take out the garbage.

Experiences like these give credibility to God's invitation to rule over sin. God's plan for cleansing and ruling over sin is on a level playing field: everyone, whether one has been a believer for sixty years or sixty minutes, has equal access to the same resources and authority. By exercising our God-given and lawful remedies over the enemy's lie-filled temptations, we call upon all the resources of heaven to come to our aid for protection and relief.

Jesus said:

> *"Very truly I tell you, everyone who sins is a slave [in bondage] to sin (John 8:34).*

> *"So if the Son sets you free, you will be free indeed" (John 8:36).*

If you are like many who struggle with sin and are at the point of discouragement, depression, and despair over your failures, tired of white-knuckling your way through life, read on. There are more pieces to this puzzle. There is a lawful basis for why these rules of engagement work. Freedom is just around the corner.

OBJECTIONS

It sounds like you are saying God controls the enemy's access to me. Does the Bible give any indication that God desires to control the enemy's access to my life?

Genesis 3 describes the encounter Eve, and later Adam, had with the enemy who disguised himself as a serpent in the garden. In Genesis 2:16-17, God instructed Adam not to eat of the Tree of Knowledge of Good and Evil. Later in Genesis 3:2-3, Eve adds that God's instruction also prohibited them from even touching the tree.[27] The best way to avoid interacting with the enemy would be for Adam and Eve to just stay clear of the tree.

---

27. Some scholars contend that Eve added the touching of the tree on her own and that touching the tree was not part of the original command. Either way, the idea is that staying away from the tree would have been the safest course of action.

It does not appear that the enemy could follow Adam and Eve around the garden and harass them. Scripture reads like the enemy was restricted to the tree, and if Adam and Eve had just stayed away from it, they would not have encountered the enemy or engaged him in conversation. By allowing themselves to get close to the tree, there was opportunity for the enemy to deceive them.

The biblical record shows that at the very beginning of human history, the enemy's access to the human race (temptation) was restricted by God to the Tree of Knowledge of Good and Evil. Moreover, the restriction would have remained in effect had they not ventured close to the tree. Unfortunately, they did wander close to the tree. They engaged with the enemy of their souls and believed his lies. This, in combination with the stories of Job, Peter, and Jesus, can lead us to a reasonable conclusion: **God will in fact limit the enemy's activity in our lives if we let *Him* manage the enemy's access to us.**

Chapter Four:

Truth and Lies

Every day we are confronted with truth and lies. We will have to decide which to embrace. The result will either lead to chaos, confusion, and conflict or freedom, peace, and joy.

Let's use the following definitions as a starting point for this discussion:

truth: "the <u>true</u> or actual state of a matter";

lie: "a false statement made with deliberate <u>intent</u> to deceive; an intentional untruth; a falsehood; something <u>intended</u> or serving to convey a false impression" (dictionary.com; emphasis mine).

This chapter puts into focus the central theme of the freedom protocol: truth and lies. Identifying the lies and truths is crucial to successfully exercising the freedom protocol. Being armed with God's truths in scripture and listening for the guidance of the Holy Spirit, we can trust that God will show us the truth and lies we've believed.

GOD IS THE EMBODIMENT OF TRUTH

There is no falsehood in God—at all. He can't lie (Heb. 6:18). When God speaks, it is true. He spoke the universe into existence, and if God said that this tree is pink—the tree would be pink. My years of personal experience and interactions with many have made this very clear: without exception, there is a lie at the root of <u>every</u> temptation. Why is this so? Because the enemy is contrary to God in every way. It is impossible for anyone, even the enemy, to be contrary to God and the truth of who He is without resorting to lies. Lies and Truth are mutually exclusive.

> *And the LORD passed by before him, and proclaimed, "The LORD, The LORD God, merciful and gracious, longsuffering, and abundant in goodness and <u>truth</u> . . ." (Exod. 34:6 KJV; emphasis mine).*

> *All the paths of the LORD are mercy and <u>truth</u> unto such as keep his covenant and his testimonies (Ps. 25:10 KJV; emphasis mine).*

> *"You are a king, then!" said Pilate. Jesus answered, "You say that I am a king. In fact, the reason I was born and came into the world is to testify to the <u>truth</u>. Everyone on the side of <u>truth</u> listens to me" (John 18:37; emphasis mine).*

THE ENEMY IS CONTRARY TO TRUTH

The enemy has no choice but to lie to distort God's truth. Therefore, he is always against God's kingdom:[28]

> *He [the man of lawlessness who gains his power from Satan] will <u>oppose</u> and will exalt himself over everything that is called God or is worshiped, so that he sets himself up in God's temple, proclaiming himself to be God (II Thess. 2:4; emphasis mine).*

THE RESULT OF BELIEVING LIES

Sin is the result when we exchange the truth of God for a lie of the enemy. Over the years no one has ever come forward with an

---

28. II Thessalonians 2:1-12. Paul describes the "man of lawlessness" (vs 3, 7-9), who receives his power from and performs the works of the enemy.

example of a temptation or sin that is not linked to a lie. Jesus said to the religious leaders of His day:

"You belong to your father, the devil, and you want to carry out your father's desires. He was a murderer from the beginning, <u>not holding to the truth</u>, for <u>there is no truth in him</u>. When he <u>lies</u>, he speaks his native language, for he is a <u>liar</u> and the <u>father of lies</u>" (John 8:44; emphasis mine).

Without fail, believing his lies will always lead to a change in our behavior and attitudes, which then leads to the outward expression of sin. For example, if I believe the lie that recreational sex is okay outside of the marriage relationship, is that belief likely to result in sinful thoughts which lead to sinful behavior and actions? Would it cause me to treat women differently or to view sex differently? Jesus said:

"You have heard that it was said, 'You shall not commit adultery.' But I tell you that anyone who looks at a woman lustfully has already committed adultery with her in his heart" (Matt. 5:27-28).

How is it that one can commit adultery in the heart before actually committing the physical act? This appears to happen when we agree with the enemy's temptation or lies. For example, before I look lustfully at a woman, I must first believe the enemy's lies, such as *she will really satisfy your desires.* When I believe that lie, it puts me into agreement with the enemy. At that moment, that agreement binds me to the enemy at the heart; even if there is no action of physical adultery taking place, there is the action of lust in the heart.

When we are tempted, there is always a crisis of belief.[29] We either believe the lies of the enemy and sin, or we embrace and

---

29. Belief, as used here, is not meant to be a theological term which might entice some to split hairs regarding its meaning as it relates to faith. Belief here means simply believ-

believe the truth as revealed by God by renouncing the lies of the enemy. In the latter case, we can successfully resist the temptation and associated sin. It always comes down to a choice, a crisis of belief. Believe the lie of the enemy, or believe the truth of God.

As a result, the following rules regarding lies and temptations are true:

- Every time we sin it is because we believe a lie of the enemy.

- When we believe a lie of the enemy, it leads to sin.

- Even if we believe a lie of the enemy about a truth of God, it leads to sin.

- It is impossible for us to sin by believing the truth.

Sin is the wickedness that results from believing the lies of the enemy; and wickedness suppresses the truth.

The wrath of God is being revealed from heaven against all the godlessness and wickedness of people, who suppress the truth by their wickedness (Rom. 1:18; emphasis mine).

They exchanged the truth about God for a lie, and worshiped and served created things rather than the Creator—who is forever praised. Amen (Rom. 1:25; emphasis mine).

Suppressing the truth is where it all starts, where sin begins. We suppress the truth by believing and agreeing with the enemy's lies.

THE ENEMY'S TACTICS

When the enemy tempts us, the foundation of that temptation is always a lie. If we believe that lie, we come into agreement with the enemy. These lies and truths are not restricted to theology or

---

ing the enemy's lies or believing God's truth. The crisis is about *whom* to believe. This is a crisis because that belief can change our eternal destiny.

biblical doctrines. They can be about anything.[30] If I suffer from low self-esteem, is there a lie in there somewhere? Am I being lied to routinely by the enemy regarding who I am? *No one likes you. You are not very smart. You do not have any talent. No one cares what you think, etc.* Would I be helped by renouncing the enemy's lies and believing the truth? It might be true that any given person is not as smart as a nuclear engineer. However, the lie about the truth will likely be *you will never achieve anything in your life because you aren't as smart as a nuclear engineer.* Notice this would be a lie about the truth. By believing this lie you would embrace a false identity and even miss your calling, living a life of frustration, anger, and defeat.

The truth is that everyone is precious to God. He can do amazing things in and through our lives if we believe the truth and see ourselves through His eyes. In the final analysis, it always comes down to a crisis of belief. A person can either believe the enemy and his lies, or choose to renounce the enemy's lies and believe the truth as revealed by their Creator. Choosing to believe the former means living in misery, defeat, and despair, whereas renouncing the enemy's lies and believing and embracing God's truth yields a life of peace, joy, victory, and freedom.

THE MULTIPLICITY OF THE ENEMY'S LIES

You may have discovered by now that it is not just one lie that binds us to the enemy on a particular issue. Generally, there are lies upon lies that we have inadvertently accepted as the truth over a number of years. While some have believed two or three lies regarding an issue, others may have believed hundreds of lies regarding the same issue. This might explain why some have less of a problem with a

---

30. In the context of *You're Invited*, truth refers to any truth whether it be about God, people, or circumstances. Every lie of the enemy, which covers a multitude of topics and issues, has a corresponding truth from God. To make truth only about theology is to miss the heart of the protocol we are discussing.

particular temptation than others, who seem to be overwhelmed by that same temptation.

When you face the mountain of lies you have believed on any issue, take heart. This process takes place in the context of your salvation, not as a means to achieve that salvation. All the while the Holy Spirit is revealing the lies and the truth to you, you can be "in Christ." Salvation is experienced in an instant. However, restoration takes time as God helps you sort out the lies from the truth for the rest of your life. Because there can be a multiplicity of lies you have believed on an issue, be careful not to settle for the first lie you find and conclude too quickly that all is well. Ask God if there are any more lies. God may reveal three or four lies, or He may reveal a hundred-fifty-two lies in a single setting as he did with one man I once counseled. He also may do the same work over a period of several years. He is in charge of your salvation and is responsible to bring you the truth in His timing. He knows just how much you can handle in the moment. The point of redemption is not to overwhelm you with your sin and the lies you may have believed but, rather, to set you free and shower you with His forgiveness and grace. Be patient and trust God to unwrap the most important lies in your life over time. He died to set you free.

Jesus said:

"Very truly I tell you, everyone who sins is a slave [in bondage] to sin" (John 8:34).

"So if the Son sets you free, you will be free indeed" (John 8:36).

OBJECTIONS

You emphasize identifying the lies of the enemy a great deal but an emphasis on devotion, submission, surrender, obedience, and trust seem to be missing.

At the heart of devotion, submission, surrender, obedience, and trust is a choice: to believe the lie or to believe the truth. Devotion to God is the byproduct of embracing the truth of who God says He is and of renouncing the enemy's lies about Him. This applies equally to *submission and surrender,* as well as to *obedience and trust.* It is impossible to believe lies about God and His character and then submit your life to Him. One might say that *obedience and trust* come from years of experience with God; but it is not necessary to take years to get to the point of trusting Him. We can start immediately to obey God, and we learn to trust Him more when we see the results of our obedience.

Below is a story my friend Gary shared with me:

I was walking the track and saw a new inmate who'd just arrived three days ago. He was half a lap ahead of me. I had been introduced to him, but had forgotten his name.

God spoke to me and said, 'Gary, go tell that man I love him.' What? I told God I do not even know the man, he's brand new, he's seventy years old, and men do not say things like that to men. God replied, 'Gary, go tell that man I love him.' Really? Come on, is this really you, God, or is it Satan trying to make a fool out of me? I tell you what, God. I'll do a fast lap to catch up with him and if he's still on the track, I will introduce myself again. And then tell him, okay? God said, 'Gary, go tell that man I love him.' I realized I was in disobedience. I immediately made a ninety-degree turn, cut across the center of the track, and walked right in front of the man. He stopped. I looked at him and said: God just told me to come tell you that He loves you. The man immediately wept, put his arms around me and said, 'I have been praying to God the last three laps asking Him why He would let this happen to me. This is an answer to my prayer.'

As we begin to obey God now, what actually happens over time is that we become convinced, little by little, that God is much different than what we had been led by the enemy to believe. This amounts to our renouncing the lies of the enemy and embracing the truth about God. Believing the truth about God and being obedient to Him builds trust, immediately and over time.

Did you spot the lies and the truths in Gary's story? When we choose to believe God, we are free to give Him our hearts with full devotion, submission, surrender, obedience, and trust.

Chapter Five:

Contracts

In chapter 3, we discussed the access rules of engagement—who has the authority to give the enemy access to my life (God and me). We grant the enemy access by believing his lies and, in doing so, we make ourselves vulnerable to his unending harassment. Remember, temptation is not a sin. But by yielding to temptations, we are agreeing with the lies of the enemy; thus, we establish an agreement regarding that lie and temptation. This chapter demonstrates that the bondage we experience as a result of granting the enemy access to our lives is akin to a lawful contract that, although binding, will only be voided by God when He can do so lawfully. We will see how God has masterfully provided the way of escape for us in every temptation.

A legal contract is a lawful agreement between two or more parties based on an offer and the acceptance of the same. Within spiritual law, an *agreement* between you and the enemy is a contract based on you accepting, or believing, his lie. In this way, we accept his proposal by agreeing with him thereby giving him permission to contract with us. Stay with me. An agreement between two or more parties with a required benefit or the hope of a benefit, also known in law as consideration, is generally all that's necessary to create a binding contract. In other words, *what's in it for us* is generally what causes us to be tempted to form a contract in the first place. The enemy's lies nearly always hold out hope for some benefit. He purports that *It will be fun*, or *Here's something to help you with your depression*, or *This will take away the pain*. When in reality, his promises are always temporary and short-lived at best.

In summation, a contract does not have to be written to be enforceable. So what constitutes my agreement to and acceptance of the enemy's contracts? My actions—they are as effective as my signature when it comes to making the contract binding. (More on this later.) Figure 3 below shows how my agreement with the enemy creates a relationship between him and me. Also note that God is not a party to my agreement with the enemy.

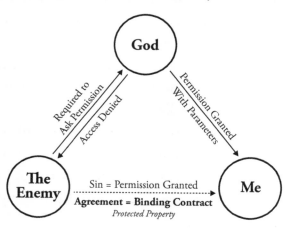

FIGURE 3. Contract formed when we grant the enemy access.

The evil deeds of the wicked ensnare them; the cords of their sins hold them fast (Prov. 5:22).

Contracts require specific elements that make them binding. I have equated these elements in law to temptations and our interactions with the enemy:

TABLE 1. Contract elements

Contract Element	Meaning Within Law	Meaning Regarding Temptation
Offer	Proposition made by the Offeror	Temptation wrapped in a lie made by the Enemy
Acceptance	Agreement with the Offeror. Generally, by means of a signature.	Agreement with the Enemy's lie. Achieved by our actions which reveal our agreement.
Consideration (benefit)	A desired outcome or the hope of a desired outcome	A promise of, what appears to be, a desired outcome. Seldom is the consideration fully realized.
Obligation	Each party is bound to perform according to the proposition and desired outcome. If a written contract, a signature is required. If unwritten, actions are required.	The Enemy binds us to performance to the offer we accepted. Since our contracts with the Enemy are unwritten, it is our actions that bind us to the contract.
Competency and Capacity	Each party has the lawful capacity to be held to a particular performance. Minors lack the competency to be bound to a contract.	The Enemy lies by promising what he cannot accomplish.

This contract requires performance. Once the above criteria are met, as we deal with the enemy of our souls, we become *bound* to him in a contract. It is not written and is somewhat intangible because you can't see it. It becomes property just like the tangible property of one's house, car, or boat. When it comes to contracts, the parties to the contract have ownership rights relative to that property created by the contract.[31] Spiritually speaking, the enemy has access rights (via property rights) to our lives, relative to the contract we created when we agreed with his temptation and lie. When we establish a contract with the enemy, God, who is always just, is not a party to this contract, which means He has no lawful rights[32] to that particular contract.

One day a good friend and I were discussing the contract elements described above and whether or not we can in fact equate the same concepts spiritually. During our discussion I expressed a thought I'd never had before, and it caught me by surprise: "If believing the enemy's lie at the time of temptation results in my establishing an agreement, or contract, with him regarding that lie, then all the principles of contract law should apply to that contract."[33] This became the revelation that led me to the freedom protocol.

---

31. When I sign a contract, the ownership rights relative to the contract do not extend to my person (body) but rather to my rights, which I may or may not have surrendered as part of the binding consideration.

32. There may be other overriding rules of engagement between God and the enemy that are not related to the permission we grant the enemy. See II Thessalonians 2:7 and Revelation 7:1. It appears that God restrains the enemy to prevent him from taking life indiscriminately. The focus here is only on the specific permission we grant the enemy.

33. References herein to "law" refer primarily to the principles of law which have been in existence for thousands of years, not a country's civil law or statutes. Civil law or statutes are generally thought to have been written to be in harmony with the age-old principles of law I am referencing.

Isn't it reasonable to consider that God, who is the Author of law, would establish in His law the remedy for the contracts we establish with the enemy? Let's unwrap this a bit more.

Thus far, we have recognized the following truths:

- Both God and I can grant the enemy access to my life:
  - When God grants the enemy access, it is always permission <u>with</u> parameters.
  - When I grant the enemy access, it is always permission <u>without</u> parameters.
- Temptation is always an integral part of the access I grant to the enemy.
- The foundation of every temptation of the enemy is always a lie.
- When I believe that lie, I come into agreement with the enemy regarding that lie.
- Agreement forms an access contract with the enemy in my life regarding that lie.
- By this established contract with the enemy, I grant him certain rights, which include unrestrained access to my life regarding that lie.
- God is not a party to the contract I have with the enemy.
- The established contract is governed by principles of contract law.
- Those principles of law were established by God thousands of years ago at the beginning of human history.

ARE CONTRACTS BINDING?

God honors the binding nature of contracts and enforces them in the spiritual realm. He certainly did when it came to the contracts and covenants[34] He formed with Adam, Noah, Abraham, Isaac, Israel, and Jesus. As we've seen, contracts delineate rights given to each party.

Rights which have been created and granted by a contract are binding and enforceable by law in nearly every government of the world. If you've ever tried to break a contract, you know this is true. The American culture we live in today does not have the same attitude toward law and contracts that our forefathers had.[35] To a large degree there is not much respect these days for property, law, rights, and contracts. People often ignore the contracts they've made with others, and many are even oblivious to the fact they've entered into a binding contract. I remember my parents saying things like *You are as good as your word,* or *Your word is your bond.* If I tell a friend I'll come by on Wednesday at 6 p.m. to help him move and I don't show up just because I changed my mind, I am, strictly speaking, in breach of a contract, and my word is not my bond. The more a society honors the principles of law in their daily activities, the more lawful that society will be. Conversely, the more a society ignores principles of law in their daily activities, the more lawless that society will become.

The enemy of our souls is described in the Bible as being the source of lawlessness:

---

34. Contracts and covenants are similar in that they both are binding and both have terms. They differ in that contracts focus more on terms as specified in the contract; while covenants focus more on relationships as seen in the issues that arise. In contracts, terms are so important that if broken, the contract generally becomes void. In covenants, relationships are more important than the agreement. If a covenant is violated, the relationship demands a resolution to keep the relationship alive.

35. In 1776, a very popular and widely read volume of books was Blackstone's *Commentary on the Laws of England.* A deeper level of understanding the law was passed down from parent to child and taught in schools for many decades. Now the law is rarely understood or taught by parents, and schools have ceased teaching law except as a discipline in college. Even law schools today do not teach the same principles of law which were taught to lawyers one hundred years ago.

For the secret power of lawlessness is already at work; but the one who now holds it back will continue to do so till he is taken out of the way. And then the lawless one will be revealed, whom the Lord Jesus will overthrow with the breath of his mouth and destroy by the splendor of his coming. The coming of the lawless one will be in accordance with how Satan works. He will use all sorts of displays of power through signs and wonders that serve the lie (II Thess. 2:7-9).

The principles of contract law are a significant part of our remedy in dealing with temptation and sin. If God's people are ignorant of these principles of law, how can they be effective in dealing with spiritual contracts in a lawful manner? Is it any wonder that the enemy is working hard to dumb down society's understanding of both secular and biblical law? A lack in understanding God's ways of dealing with sin affects our knowledge and ability to exercise the remedies He's put in place for us to effectively and predictably rule over sin.

CAN CONTRACTS BE BROKEN?

There is no evidence in scripture that *God* grants the enemy unrestrained access to tempt and harass anyone.[36] Scripture makes it clear that when God grants the enemy access to my life it is always with parameters:

No temptation has overtaken you except what is common to mankind. And God is faithful; he will not <u>let</u> you be tempted <u>beyond what you can bear</u>. But when you are tempted, he will <u>also provide a way out</u> so that you can endure it (I Cor. 10:13; emphasis mine).

---

36. In Job chapters 1 and 2, it may appear that God has granted the enemy unrestricted access to Job. However, there were limitations in the parameters: "You can't touch him," and "You can't kill him."

If I am harassed and tormented by the enemy on any issue, this should be my first clue that I have contractually granted him access. When I'm the one granting permission, I'm open and vulnerable to his harassment with no parameters. Once I recognize this, my next thought should be, "Lord, where is the contract? What is the lie I believed?" In other words, when we are tormented by the enemy and suspect that an access point exists, we can ask God to identify it. He will reveal the lie that deceived us into making the contract. We are now a step closer to lawfully breaking the contract and being set free from its bondage.

The lies may be tricky to identify at first, but the more practiced we become at dealing with this aspect of temptation, the easier it becomes to spot them. Victory can happen more quickly than you might expect. It is emancipating to catch the enemy with his hand in the cookie jar, so to speak. I have had people tell me that they actually laughed out loud when they caught the enemy lying to them.

THE KEY TO BREAKING CONTRACTS

Listed below are specific ways, or vitiating factors, in which a contract can legally be broken. As you read, think about aspects of biblical law and how they relate to aspects of common law:
A contract is *void* for these reasons:

- The terms of the agreement are illegal (unlawful consideration or purpose).

- A party was not of sound mind when the agreement was signed.

- A party was under the age of consent.

- The terms are impossible.

- The contract restricts the rights of a party to the contract.

CONTRACTS   55

A contract is *voidable* under the following circumstances:

- A party was coerced or threatened into signing the agreement.

- A party was under undue influence (one party is able to control the will of another).

- A party is not of sound mind or mentally competent (minor or mentally ill).

- The terms of the contract were breached.

- Mutual mistakes on behalf of both parties.

- The contract is fraudulent (omitting or falsifying facts or information, or the intention is to not carry out the promise in the contract).

- Misrepresentation occurs (a false statement of fact).

Remedies for these circumstances can break or make voidable a contract:

Misrepresentation in any contract entered into by two or more parties vitiates (impairs the legal validity of) that contract "ab initio" (from the beginning).[37]

An example of this rule of law happens to be codified in Arizona Revised Statutes, Title 44 § 1797.13, and is quoted in part as follows:

Any untrue or misleading information, representation, notice, material omission . . . which has been received by or made to the buyer before he signs a contract . . . renders the contract . . . void and unenforceable by the seller.[38]

---

37. Leaf v International Galleries, [1950] 2 KB 86

38. Ariz. Rev. Stat. § 44-1797-13. "Misrepresentation; contract void and unenforceable." https://www.azleg.gov/arsDetail/?title=44. (8/17/2019).

The rules of engagement in this book are based on the very idea of *misrepresentations,* or lies. Since every temptation and resulting access contract we grant to the enemy is <u>always</u> based on a lie, any such contract is voidable *ab initio (to the beginning)* as soon as we renounce the lie, embrace the truth, and repent of the contract and the lie that established it. Then, God can and will void that contract in a lawful manner and without trespassing on the enemy's property rights. Let me illustrate this further with some examples.

CONTRACT EXAMPLES

MARRIAGE CONTRACT

Let's say you marry the love of your life. Five years and two children later, you discover your husband was married before your marriage, only he never got a divorce. What does this do to your marriage? Once the truth is discovered, your marriage is lawfully and legally void *ab initio*; [39] it never happened. What does this make your children? Illegitimate.[40] Such is the power of law. One minute you are happily married under a contract of marriage with two children and the next, no contract ever existed, you were never married, and you have two illegitimate children—all due to the lie that was foundational to your marriage contract. The ripple effect is great, encompassing not just the marriage partners, but the children, the rights of inheritance, and extended family.

---

39. Some say that a contract established on a lie is voidable and *not* void; in the above example, the marriage is legally and lawfully defendable until the truth is learned. At that moment, the marriage is void because that contract can no longer be defended legally and lawfully. It does not require a court decision for the marriage to be void; as soon as it becomes indefensible in a legal proceeding, it is void. In other words, the marriage contract was a valid contract until the truth and the lie became known. At that time, the marriage became void; it never happened. In addition, all relationships related to this voided marriage are also changed (i.e., the children, in-laws, etc.).

40. This would be true in law and under common law for thousands of years. Today, the law has been changed to assume a presumption of legitimacy.

As you ponder the contracts you may have established with the enemy over the years, ask God to reveal them and their underlying lies. Prayerfully seek the truth in each case so you can repent and renounce the lies and make the contracts voidable, choosing instead to believe and embrace the truth.

PORNOGRAPHY CONTRACT

One afternoon I walked in on Fred while he was reading a "light" pornography magazine. Fred is a believer, and I asked him, "Why are you engaged in looking at pornography?"

Fred immediately expressed a list of suggestions (lies) he had heard the enemy say to him over the years: It's not really hard pornography; it's no big deal—looking at the light stuff is okay; women are beautiful and have been created by God to be looked at.

I then spent a few minutes explaining the freedom protocol to him as it related to pornography. We subsequently moved on to discuss other topics, and then I left. About three weeks later Fred pulled me aside and told me he had spent some quality time with God on the pornography issue. He asked God to show him the lies he'd believed over the years and said that God took him all the way back to age twelve.

"Do you know how many lies and contracts I discovered?" Fred said.

I told him I didn't know and asked him how many he'd found.

"The Lord showed me fifty-two lies and contracts I have formed with the enemy over the years," Fred said.

I told him that he and God had already done the heavy lifting. Now all he had to do was repent (change his mind), renounce each lie and resulting contract, and believe and embrace God's truth. In doing this, God would void those contracts, and Fred would be free from the enemy's harassing temptations on that issue.

Fred took a prayer I gave him and prayed through each lie and contract. He was set free.

Rest assured, if you are serious about dealing with the lies and contracts in your life, God is faithful and will show you the path to freedom.

ACCUSATION CONTRACT

Rick and Irene were in my office for marriage counseling. When Irene smiled at Rick he immediately became angry then looked at me: "For the past thirty years she has repeatedly looked at me with that cynical smile." I asked Rick if he was certain Irene meant to be cynical when she smiled at him. He said "No." I asked him what he thought he should do since he was unsure of Irene's intent behind her smile. Rick came to the conclusion he should actually ask Irene what her intent was, rather than just assume.

"Were you being cynical when you smiled at me just now?" Rick said.

"No," Irene said.

"Have your smiles over the past thirty years been meant to be cynical?"

"No, not at all."

The enemy had robbed Rick of the joy of Irene's smiles for thirty years.

Rick immediately took Irene's hands. He repented of his accusations, renounced the lie that had gripped him for so many years, and embraced the truth that when Irene smiled at him, it was genuine and not meant to be cynical.

The next day at 3:30 a.m., Rick was up working on some of his homework for counseling. In a moment, he saw in his mind's eye his wife's smile and started to have the same reaction of anger as the day before. Immediately, the Holy Spirit reminded him that he was no longer bound by that lie. Instead of agreeing with the enemy's lie, he agreed with the Holy Spirit—and was instantly set free from that harassing thought from the enemy.

As soon as we recognize a contract and its associated lie, we can immediately and lawfully exercise the freedom protocol. Jesus invites us to obtain freedom from the enemy's harassment and to make every effort to deny the enemy unrestricted access to our lives and hearts.

When we agree with God and believe and embrace the truth, we come into contract with Him and immediately establish ourselves under His protection. Now, God can lawfully stand at the door of our hearts to limit and regulate the enemy's access.

Chapter Six:

Ruling Over Sin

This chapter is the hinge pin that connects the freedom protocol to the remaining chapters in part one. Without an understanding of God's expectation regarding sin, we have little confidence that ruling over sin is something we should pursue. Genesis 4:7 is the lens we'll use to read accounts in scripture of God's interaction with His creation.

What is God's expectation for us regarding sin? The easy answer is that He does not want us to sin at all. It was certainly God's desire for Adam and Eve not to sin. What about now? How does God want mankind to relate to sin from now until Jesus returns? Genesis records God talking to Cain, and He makes a very interesting statement:

> *"If you do well, will not your countenance be lifted up? And if you do not do well, sin is crouching at the door; and its desire is for you, but you must <u>master</u> it" (Gen. 4:7 NASB; emphasis mine).*

God's plan for mankind at the beginning of human history is that we "master" sin. Other translations use the term "rule over." In either case it does not appear that God expects us to be relentlessly pushed around and harassed by the enemy's temptations and our sin. In fact, the opposite is true—Genesis 4:7 says that we *should rule* over it. In the verse above, the grammatical context related to the Hebrew verb "must master," in other versions "should rule," is a

TABLE 2. God's remedies

	#	Remedies	Meaning of Remedies
S A L V A T I O N	1	Deliverance from the **Pollution** of Sin	This deliverance occurs when we receive Jesus as Lord and Savior. Receiving Him means we have eternal life in Jesus and no matter how sinful our past, we are cleansed in a moment of all our sin. (I John 1:7; I John 5:11-12)
	2	Deliverance from the **Power** of Sin	This deliverance occurs between the time we receive Jesus as Lord and the second coming of Jesus. This is the time when God expects us to be overcomers and to rule over sin. (Rom. 8:2)
	3	Deliverance from the **Presence** of Sin	At Jesus' second coming He saves the righteous and removes them from the very presence of sin. (John 14:1-3)
	4	Deliverance from the **Propensity** to Sin	Also at Jesus' return, those still living on the earth, who have struggled with their sinful nature for so many years, are changed in a moment and are delivered from their sinful nature and propensity to sin. (I Cor. 15:52)
	5	Deliverance from the **Pronouncement** of Sin	After the second coming and the thousand-year millennium, there is the great white throne judgment where the wicked are judged and publicly pronounced guilty of sin and sentenced to the penalty of second death in the lake of fire. (Rev. 20:11)
	6	Deliverance from the **Penalty** of Sin	Following the judgment, the wicked receive the penalty for sin. They are destroyed and perish in the lake of fire. This is the second death. The wages of sin is death. (Rev. 21:8, Rom. 6:23)
	7	Deliverance from the **Possibility** of Sin	After the wicked are punished and destroyed, God creates a new heaven and a new earth where all traces of sin have been eliminated from God's universe, and there is no possibility of sin ever returning again. (I Thess. 5:23)

command. This command is not given to add burdens to our lives, but to encourage us. How? Because a just God would not ask something of us and not provide a means to do it. Let's start with what God has already given us: remedies.

GOD'S REMEDIES

The word remedy is defined as "a means of counteracting or eliminating something undesirable" and "the means employed to enforce a right or redress an injury."[41]

When we give our lives to Jesus as Lord and Savior, not only is there a deliverance (remedy) from the *pollution* of sin, there is also a deliverance from the *power* of sin that allows us to actually rule over sin.[42] Notice table 3 below shows the first four remedies we saw in table 2 above.

TABLE 3. Remedies timeline

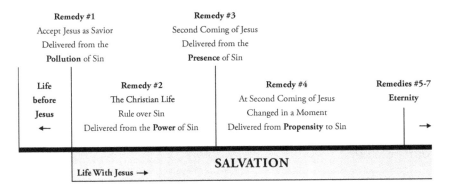

---

41. *Bouvier's Law Dictionary and Concise Encyclopedia: Volume 3*, s.v. "remedy" (p. 2870), accessed August 16, 2017, https://goo.gl/eZgtL9.

42. Even before one gives their life to Jesus Christ, they can experience some freedom. Your freedom depends on the amount and quality of the truth you are embracing. Jesus Christ is the way, the *truth* and the life. God shows His love toward us by giving us some peace and protection even before we surrender our lives to Him.

In reviewing table 3 above, can you see how God provides the remedy for us to have victory over the power of sin while we await Jesus' return?

God presents Himself in scripture as the One who is always perfectly just. If ruling over sin is God's expectation for our lives, then a perfectly just God must provide us with the remedies to successfully meet His expectations. It would be profoundly unjust for God to expect us to rule over sin and then fail to provide us a remedy and show us the way to freedom.

FUNDAMENTAL RULES OF COMMON LAW

In order to understand God's remedies that give us victory over the power of sin, we'll take a deeper look at the character of God related to justice and His command to rule over sin. But first, let's take a look at aspects of justice not often addressed with respect to God and His character.

We see remedies within federal and state law and follow a process (protocol) to access remedies that have been designed by legislators to provide us with relief.

Any valid and just law must be reasonable, good for all, and not merely for the benefit of a few. A good example of this in common law is from Chief Justice Coke in England in 1610 when the Coke court ruled that

> *in many cases the common law will control acts of Parliament and sometime adjudge them to be utterly void: for when an act of Parliament is against common right or reason, or repugnant, or* <u>*impossible to be performed*</u>*, the common law will control it and adjudge such an Act to be void*[43] *(emphasis mine).*

---

43. Thomas Bonham v. College of Physicians, (1610) 8 Co. Rep. 107. I cite English Common Law because it is clear and concise. What Coke said of Parliament can also be

A law that is impossible to perform is unlawful and unjust. If a person is starving, then a law forbidding him to work is unlawful. This principle of law was confirmed years later in the case of *Thomas v Sorrell (1673)* [44] when the court ruled

> *a law which a man cannot obey, nor act according to it, is void and no law; and it is impossible to obey contradictions, or act according to them.*

Since it is a fundamental rule of law that it is unlawful to create a law which is unreasonable or one which is impossible to obey,[45] God, even as the creator of law, would be unjust if He demanded that we do something He knows is impossible.[46] In over fifty places in scripture, God says, "Keep my statutes and commands," "Keep my statutes and ordinances," "Keep my commands," and "Keep my commandments." Either God is unjust to expect the impossible or He is just to expect the possible.

We are not capable of resisting sin in our own strength, and we certainly do not have the ability in ourselves to resist the onslaught of the enemy's relentless and harassing temptations. The answer to the chasm between *God's expectations to rule over sin* and *our abilities* must, then, lie in a clearer understanding of the remedies which God as the Author of law has established to meet His expectations.

---

said of Congress and State legislatures. Fundamental principles of law never go out of style in a lawful society.

44. Thomas v. Sorrel, (1673) Vaugh 330.

45. When the apostle Paul speaks of not being able to keep the law, he's discussing salvation and, in that context, he's speaking of perfect law-keeping not just keeping the law from now on. (See Galatians 3:10.) Even if I keep the law perfectly from today on, that does not solve the problem of my past law-breaking which disqualifies me from eternal life. "For whoever keeps the whole law and yet stumbles at just one point is guilty of breaking all of it" (James 2:10). For the purpose of salvation, law-keeping demands 100 percent, perfect compliance with all the demands of the law. For the purpose of obedience to God's commands from now on, He only commands what we can do.

46. It's worth noting here that it was after sin entered the world that God told Cain to rule over sin.

Ruling over sin is about obedience to God and His ways. It's not about our strength but God's authority and protection. God makes it possible for us to obey His commands and to be free of harassing temptations of the enemy. What are we ruling when we rule over sin?

Chapter Seven:

What Is Sin?

There are many definitions of sin and many have attempted to define it. When I was much younger, I saw a rather large book entitled *Sin*, and although I don't remember the author's name, I do remember how the mere appearance of it affected me. I didn't think I wanted to know that much about sin. But it would be difficult to move forward to freedom without knowing what it is we need to break free from. This chapter considers three aspects of sin: sinful nature, sinful actions, and sinful intent. This is not an attempt to present an exhaustive study but, rather, a means to examine what the Bible says about sin in the context of God's expectations. While this chapter may seem to be a bit technical, it includes truths that will be important as you personally implement the freedom protocol.

Many authors and theologians, in the interest of emphasizing the gravity of sin, tend to go beyond what the Bible actually defines as sin—and they inadvertently create a type of sin that is impossible to rule over as God expects and directs. While these authors might mean well, it does little to encourage the sinner in their attempt to honor God by their obedience. And if we go beyond what the Bible says in an attempt to deal with sin, we will create problems elsewhere. It is always best to only go as far as the Bible goes in defining sin and not add a severity to it that has not been established by God in scripture.

First things first—we are all born with a sinful nature. The question is does God punish us for having a sinful nature, a nature He allows to exist within us?

It is quite clear that we all have a sin problem. In our very nature we have a propensity to sin (as seen in Romans 7 below). Finding righteousness in us is like someone trying to get a fresh, cool drink from a polluted well. They do their best to push aside the debris but try as they may, it is still polluted and discouraging.

Even so, nowhere in the Bible are the wicked punished because they have a sinful nature. Can a just God allow our natures to be sinful, generation after generation, as a result of the fall of Adam, and then punish us for having that sinful nature? Or can a just God punish us for Adam's sin? [47]

> *The one who sins is the one who will die. The child will not share the guilt of the parent, nor will the parent share the guilt of the child. The righteousness of the righteous will be credited to them, and the wickedness of the wicked will be charged against them (Ezek. 18:20).*

The enemy wants nothing more than to discourage sinners from attempting to rule over sin in their lives. If he can just convince us that we can never please or obey God or live according to God's plan for the human race, then he will keep us continually defeated and discouraged.

---

47. Adam became subject to physical death primarily because he no longer had access to the tree of life. We are subject to physical death for the same reason. There is a second death at the end of the world that will affect those who have rejected the tender pleadings of the Savior. That death is more than just a physical death experienced by people of all ages. That death separates the wicked from God for eternity.

Paul, in Romans 7, discusses in detail the struggle and disappointment he has in dealing with the sinful nature. These verses also have a dramatic impact on intent and actions which we will discuss shortly.

We know that the law is spiritual; but I am unspiritual, sold as a slave to sin [sinful nature]. I do not understand what I do. For what I want to do [intent] I do not do [action], but what I hate [intent] I do [action]. And if I do [action] what I <u>do not want to do</u> [intent], I agree that the law is good. As it is, it is no longer I myself who do it [action], but it is sin living in me [action without intent – no culpability]. For I know that good itself does not dwell in me, that is, in <u>my sinful nature</u>. For I have the desire [intent] to do what is good, but I cannot carry it out [action]. For I do not do [action] the good I want to do [intent], but the evil I do not want to do [intent]—this I keep on doing [action without intent – no culpability]. Now if I do [action] what I do not want to do [intent], <u>it is no longer I who do it</u> [action without intent], but it is sin living in me that does it [action without intent—no culpability] (Rom. 7:14-20; emphasis mine).

Everyone who desires to live for God has experienced these emotions described by Paul. However, Paul is not suggesting that one is lost because of their sinful nature, and he is not suggesting that God will punish one for having a sinful nature. In fact, Paul makes it clear that his intent is to honor God by not willingly participating in the desires of his nature.

Clearly, we are not punished because we have a sinful nature, and we are not punished for Adam's sin.[48] Yet, since it is clear that

---

48. It is true that we became subject to death as a result of Adam's sin, but this is not the same as being punished for Adam's sin. If we are punished for sin, we will only be punished for our sin (Ezek. 18:20).

God does and will punish sin, let's unwrap what the Bible says about the actions that rise to the level of sin which God *will* punish in the end.

A BIBLICAL RECORD OF SINS THAT GOD PUNISHED

One way to understand sin is to examine examples of what God punishes as sin in the biblical record. We might come up with many scenarios that a reasonable person would call sin, but what does the Bible actually claim is a sin and that which makes us culpable? In the following biblical records, consider what God shows as punishable to discover basic reasons why some actions *we would call* sin rise to the level of a punishable act, and some do not.

Below are examples of those who were punished by God for their actions:

TABLE 4. Actions punished

Meaning Within Law Actions Punished by God	Scripture Reference
Adam and Eve eat forbidden fruit	Genesis 3
Cain murders his brother Able	Genesis 4
Sodom and Gomorrah commit grievous sin	Genesis 18-19
Lot's wife looks back to Sodom	Genesis 19:26
Israel worships a golden calf	Exodus 32
Abihu and Nadab offer strange fire in the temple	Leviticus 10
Twenty-four-thousand Israelites practice immorality and Baal worship	Numbers 25
Saul disobeys God by not destroying the Amalekites	I Samuel 15
King David takes a census	II Samuel 24

There are also examples of those who acted in what many would call sinful ways and yet, God did not punish them for their actions:

TABLE 5. Actions not punished

Actions Not Punished by God	Scripture Reference
Lot is selfish and takes the best land	Genesis 13
Abraham and Sarah distrust God for His promise of their first son, Ishmael	Genesis 16
Abraham lies about Sarah being his sister	Genesis 20
Isaac lies about Rebekah being his sister	Genesis 26
Moses murders an Egyptian	Exodus 2
Rahab lies to searching guards	Joshua 2

It does seem odd to see some actions we might consider sin, even today, not punishable, or even acknowledged by God, while others definitely are. Because God is just in all His ways, what is it about these actions that cause a just God to ignore them? While some might argue what should or shouldn't be punishable by God, the first group of actions above, table 4, is clearly about individuals being punished for their actions. The second group, table 5, is about those who acted in ways we would consider sinful but yet, they were not punished for their actions. As we dig a bit deeper, principles of law will give us guidance regarding why God punishes some actions and does not punish others.

ACTUS REUS AND MENS REA

The Latin words *actus reus* (actions) and *mens rea* (intent) form a part of a larger phrase in common law: "*Actus reus non facit reum nisi mens sit rea,*" which means "the act is not culpable unless the mind is guilty." Let's unpack this phrase in law for the purpose of obtaining a clearer understanding of sin in the biblical context.

In law, for an action (*actus reus*) to rise to the level of a crime, it requires a combination of both the action (*actus reus*) and the intent (*mens rea*).

In the three aspects of sin we're discussing (sinful nature, actions, and intent), which does God actually punish? As we saw in table 4, there is evidence that God certainly will, and does, punish actions that are contrary to His commands. As you read the Bible, you will find many more examples of those who were punished for their actions. Now let's look at intent (*mens rea*).

Nehemiah describes how a temptation to believe a lie (to become frightened) joined to an action constitutes sin:

> *He was hired for this reason, that **I might become frightened [believe a lie] and act accordingly [an action] and sin**, so that they might have an evil report in order that they could reproach me (Neh. 6:13 NASB; emphasis mine).*

When we believe a lie of the enemy, our intent comes into harmony with that lie. When we believe the truth of God, our intent comes into harmony with that truth.

Nehemiah records that it takes two elements to cause an action to rise to the level of a sin: the action *(actus reus)—act accordingly;* and the intent *(mens rea)—become frightened.* Both are required before one can be punished of any action deemed a sin. As seen in the examples of actions punished in table 4, it is clear that the actions were punished by God—what is not always clearly recorded is the *intent* of those who were punished. Is intent *(mens rea)* always required by God before He punishes a person's actions as sin? Let's look at some examples where God speaks about the issue of intent.

Genesis 6 records what the world was like just prior to Noah's flood:

> *The Lord saw how great the wickedness [actions] of the human race had become on the earth, and that every inclination of the thoughts*

of the human heart [intent] was <u>only evil</u> <u>all the time</u> (Gen. 6:5; emphasis mine).

God states quite clearly that it was because of their <u>actions</u> and <u>intent</u> being <u>only evil all the time</u> that He punished the world by a catastrophic flood about 2,000 years after creation. He saved only eight people. This shows that God's actions against the world were just and lawful because everyone who was not saved not only acted wickedly but their *intent* was "only evil all the time."

And after the flood, God states:

"Never again will I curse the ground because of humans, even though every inclination of the human heart [intent] is evil from childhood. . . ." (Gen. 8:21b).

"As for you, my son Solomon, know the God of your father, and serve Him with a whole heart and a willing mind; for the LORD searches all hearts, and understands every intent of the thoughts. . . ." (I Chron. 28:9 NASB).

Throughout the Bible, God shows us that intent is very important to Him.

The steadfast of mind [intent] You will keep in perfect peace, because he trusts in You (Isa. 26:3 NASB).

The writer of Hebrews also ties intent to sin:

If we deliberately [intent] keep on sinning [actions] after we have received the knowledge of the truth, no sacrifice for sins is left, but only a fearful expectation of judgment and of raging fire that will consume the enemies of God (Heb. 10:26-27).

This helps us understand what the Apostle John means when he states:

No one who lives in him keeps on sinning [intent + actions] (I John 3:6a).

My dear children, I write this to you so that you will not sin [intent + action]. But if anybody does sin, we have an advocate with the Father—Jesus Christ, the Righteous One (I John 2:1).

We know that anyone born of God does not continue to sin [intent + actions]; the One who was born of God keeps them safe, and the evil one cannot harm them (I John 5:18).

As we view the list of those who were not punished for their actions, deciphering the intent in each example might give us some understanding as to what rises to the level of culpable sin in God's eyes. In some situations, their actions may have had an intent such as self-defense. In others, like the story of Lot (Genesis 13), he did exactly what Abraham told him he could do, and even though he was selfish about taking the best land for himself (intent), Lot's actions were not punished because they were lawful and in accordance with Abraham's wishes and directions. With regard to Moses killing the Egyptian, his intent appears to be one of protecting his people, a defensive posture. He may have thought this was how God was going to free Israel from the bondage of Egypt. Throughout the biblical record, it doesn't appear that having an incorrect understanding is a sin. Therefore, Moses was not punished as Cain was punished in Genesis 4 for taking another's life.

James describes the progression of the life of sin from temptation to death:

When tempted, no one should say, "God is tempting me." For God cannot be tempted by evil, nor does he tempt anyone; but each person is tempted when they are dragged away by their own evil desire [sinful nature] and enticed [deceived by the enemy's lies]. Then, after desire [intent] has conceived [turns into action], it gives birth to sin [punishable]; and sin, when it is full-grown, gives birth to death [wages of sin]. Don't be deceived [believe the enemy's lies], my dear brothers and sisters (James 1:13-16).

The birth of sin happens only after the sinful nature (desire) and the enemy's temptation (lies) result in an action, which is then called sin. The solution to this pathway to sin is a foundation of our thesis: it takes both intent and action to become guilty.

Don't be deceived [believe the enemy's lies], my dear brothers and sisters (James 1:16).

In his letter to the Romans, Paul presents nearly the same progression from temptation to sin and death that James makes when he states:

For when we were in the realm of the flesh, the sinful passions [sinful nature] aroused by the law were at work in us, so that we bore fruit [intent + actions = sin] for death [wages of sin] (Rom. 7:5).

Because the Word of God is all we need to determine how to live for Him, it stands to reason that His Word would show us what culpable sin is by showing us what He punishes as sin. From this perspective, and from looking in God's Word for evidence to the contrary, it is safe to conclude that

- God punishes evil actions which are contrary to His will and commands.

- God punishes those evil actions as sin, only when the intent is evil as well.

- God does not punish evil intent when not accompanied with evil actions. (Note: intent, here, is not to be confused with covetousness. To covet, although it sounds like an intent without an action, is a different meaning. More on this later.)

- God does not punish anyone for having a sinful nature.

Since God is the author of law and principles of law that have existed since the beginning of human history, it is reasonable to conclude that the uniting of **Intent + Actions** in common law would also be found in biblical law as follows:

Evil Intent + Evil Actions = Sin

There is one more element to intent: knowledge. Knowledge and intent are inseparably tied. It is impossible to have intent without having knowledge first, and James makes this clear when he states the following:

> *If anyone, then, knows the good they ought to do [knowledge/intent] and doesn't do it [action], it is sin [intent + action = sin] for them"* (James 4:17).

> *What causes fights and quarrels among you? Don't they come from your desires [sinful nature] that battle within you? You desire [intent] but do not have, so you kill [intent + action = sin]. You covet [action] but you cannot get what you want [intent], so you quarrel and fight [intent + actions = sin]. You do not have because you do not ask God. When you ask, you do not receive, because you ask [action] with wrong motives [intent], that you may spend what you get [action] on your pleasures [intent + action = sin]* (James 4:1-3).

Paul also confirms this same understanding:

> *For until the Law sin was in the world: but sin is not imputed when there is no law [notice of what is sin or knowledge]* (Rom. 5:13 NASB).

> *Those who want to get rich [intent] fall into temptation and a trap [believe the enemy's lies] and into many foolish and harmful desires [nature given way to intent] that plunge people into ruin and destruction [intent + actions = sin]* (I Tim. 6:9).

We've seen from scripture that God punishes evil actions that are contrary to His will and commands. What is more difficult to see from the biblical record is that every evil action punished by God also included an evil intent. Intent is not easy to determine when the Bible often leaves out some details and makes some assumptions about who God is. Since many of the biblical authors openly declare that God is perfectly just, there is no need to show each time that the one who was punished had evil intent and that God was just in punishing them. If the biblical record shows that God punishes individuals for their actions when there is no evil intent, then we must, of necessity, either reevaluate God's declaration in the Bible that He is perfectly just or reevaluate our thesis that it takes both intent and action to become guilty of sin, even if intent is not clearly stated.

If there is no lawful order to God's definition of what constitutes sin, then it will be impossible to rule over sin in one's life; it would be a moving and impossible target. Also, if there is no lawful order to God's definition of what constitutes sin, and what is proposed here is not true, then this would make God arbitrary and capricious in dealing with sin, and His perfectly just nature could be called into question. If our thesis is *not* true, then it should be easy to find specific examples in the Bible where

- God punishes evil actions even when there is clearly no evil intent;
- God punishes evil intent alone without any accompanied evil actions; and
- God punishes sinners just for having a sinful nature.

ACTION AND INTENT IN THE TEN COMMANDMENTS

It is quite clear in the ten commandments that each commandment involves an action of some sort. Even the first commandment

("Thou shall have no other gods before Me," Deuteronomy 5:6) implies an action whereby one replaces the living God with anything or anyone else. By doing so, God is replaced (action) in the heart by a lesser god.

However, the tenth commandment appears to cause some difficulty:

> *"You shall not covet your neighbor's house. You shall not covet your neighbor's wife, or his male or female servant, his ox or donkey, or anything that belongs to your neighbor" (Exod. 20:17).*

On the surface, this appears to be referring to one's emotions or an inner impulse and not to an action. If our thesis is correct, then there must be some indication that to covet is not only a thought process but an evil action. This action, combined with evil intent, constitutes sin. To get a better understanding of what covetousness involves, let's examine this commandment more closely.

WHAT IS COVETOUSNESS?

The word for "covet" in the Hebrew is דמח ("hamad"). Von Rad writes regarding the word "covet":

> *If in the last commandment the translation of the verb as 'covet' were correct, it would be the only case in which the Decalogue deals not with an action, but with an inner impulse, hence with a sin of intention. But the corresponding Hebrew word (hamad) has two meanings, both to covet and to take. It includes outward malpractices, meaning seizing for oneself (Josh. 7:21, Mic. 2:2).[49]*

Adam Clarke gives even more clarity by his comments about the word "covet":

> *Thou shalt not covet, ver. 17 . . . lo tachemod—the word chamad, signifies an earnest and strong desire after a matter, on which all the*

---

49. Von Rad, Gerhard. *Deuteronomy, a Commentary*, Westminster Press, 1966, p. 59.

affections are concentrated and fixed, whether the thing be good or bad. This is what we commonly term covetousness, which word is taken both in a good and a bad sense. So when the scripture says, that covetousness is idolatry: yet it also says, covet earnestly the best things; so we find that this disposition is sinful or holy, according to the object on which it is fixed.[50]

Covetousness is generally thought of as a word that describes evil, but Clark observes that to "covet" can be either good or bad depending on the object to which it is attached.

Clarke continues:

He breaks the command, who by any means endeavours to deprive a man of his house, or farm, by some underhanded and clandestine bargain with the original landlord; what is called in some countries, taking a man's house and farm over his head. He breaks it also, who lusts after his neighbour's wife, and endeavours to ingratiate himself into her affections, by striving to lessen her husband in her esteem: he who feels the force of the law which prohibits the inordinate desire of anything that is the property of another, can never make a breach in the peace of society by an act of wrong to any of even its feeblest members.[51]

Clarke is describing evil actions aimed at acquiring the coveted object or person.

COVET—INTENT AND/OR ACTION

"You know the commandments, 'DO NOT MURDER, DO NOT COMMIT ADULTERY, DO NOT STEAL, DO NOT BEAR

50. Adam Clarke, *Discourses on Various Subjects, Vol.* II (1831): 36, quoted in Rousas John Rushdoony, *The Institutes of Biblical Law* (Presbyterian and Reformed Publishing Co., 1973) p. 633.

51. Adam Clarke, *Discourses on Various Subjects, Vol.* II (1831): 36, quoted in Rousas John Rushdoony, *The Institutes of Biblical Law* (Presbyterian and Reformed Publishing Co., 1973) p. 633.

FALSE WITNESS, do not defraud,[52] *HONOR YOUR FATHER AND MOTHER'" (Mark 10:19 NASB).*

In Mark 10:19, Jesus is speaking to the rich, young ruler. When He says, "Do not defraud," He is referring to the word "covet" in the context of the tenth commandment. This is not the same meaning as "stealing" from the eighth commandment mentioned earlier in the same verse. Notice in the Old Testament scriptures regarding the Ten Commandments, the first four commandments refer to mankind's relationship with God. In this passage, Mark 10, Jesus includes all six of the last six commandments which are applicable to our relationships with others. Clearly Jesus is using the word defraud in the context of an action, given its meaning and the question the rich, young ruler asked: What must I *do* to inherit eternal life?

The great Anglican scholar of the 17th century, Dr. Isaac Barrow, writing on the tenth commandment, observed this:

> *The law is comprehensive and recapitulatory, as it were, of the rest concerning our neighbor, prescribing universal justice toward him (whence St. Mark, it seems, meaneth to render it in one word, by ... deprive not, or bereave not your neighbor of anything; Mark x.19) and this not only in outward deed and dealing, but in inward thought and desire, the spring whence they do issue forth.*[53]

Paul in his letter to Corinth, used the word "covet" in its good sense:

> *But covet earnestly the best gifts . . . (I Cor. 12:31 KJV).*

Paul is not just speaking of a desire but of the active acquiring of the best gifts.

---

52. *Defraud* means to defraud, deprive of, rob, despoil.
Strong's Concordance, s.v. "650: defraud." https://biblehub.com/greek/650.htm.
53. *The Works of Isaac Barrow* (1845): 39, quoted in Rousas John Rushdoony, *The Institutes of Biblical Law* (Presbyterian and Reformed Publishing Co., 1973) p. 633.

THE LINE BETWEEN INTENT AND ACTION

The line between intent and action can sometimes be difficult to determine. Remember that we are looking at intent and action in the context of ruling over sin. In Romans 7, Paul describes certain desires rising up within us that we despise and wish didn't exist in our lives. He states that we are not culpable for our sinful natures ("As it is, it is no longer I myself who do it, but it is sin living in me."). When we <u>nurture</u> the sinful nature and its desires, we have crossed the line from intent only to intent + action, even if that action is not observable by others.

In the sermon on the mount, Jesus states:

> *"You have heard that it was said, 'You shall not commit adultery.' But I tell you that anyone who looks at a woman <u>lustfully</u> has al-ready committed adultery with her in his heart" (Matt. 5:27-28; emphasis mine).*

How you view this verse depends on your view of the word lust. Paul in discussing lust makes an important point, which is captured by the KJV:

> *What shall we say then? Is the law sin? God forbid. Nay, I had not known sin, but by the law: for I had not known lust,[54] except the law had said, 'Thou shalt not covet[55] (Rom. 7:7 KJV).*

The KJV makes a valid distinction between the two Greek words to convey "lust" and "covet." Paul equates lust with coveting. As we have pointed out above, to covet means more than just having a desire or even an intent. It is far more than just desiring another

---

54. *The Complete Word Study Dictionary: New Testament.* (AMG International, Inc., 1992), s.v. "lust." ἐπιθυμία ("epithumia"), a carnal desire, Spiros Zodhiates.

55. *The Complete Word Study Dictionary: New Testament.* (AMG International, Inc., 1992), s.v. "covet." ἐπιθυμέω ("epithumeō"), strong desire, Zodhiates.

person. If we apply the meaning of covetousness as described above to the counsel of Jesus and Paul, both are arguably referring to those instances where one has crossed the line from intent to action, however slight or unnoticeable that action might be to others.

Jesus' focus is always on the heart. He counsels to forgive from the heart (Matt. 18:35), and not to commit adultery in our hearts (Matt. 5:27-28). Solomon gives us good counsel when he states:

> *Above all else, guard your heart, for everything you do flows from it (Prov. 4:23).*

We are counseled to guard our hearts because everything (actions and sin) flows from our hearts (intent). Is it God's expectation that we rule over lust and covetousness in our lives? What Paul and Jesus are referring to are not the overwhelming desires of our sinful nature but the setting of our hearts (intent) on sin, so much so that out of our hearts flow evil intent that results in evil actions (sin: intent + actions). It appears that Jesus is referring to one who has crossed the line with purpose in his heart, to embrace and act upon what God declares to be sin.

BELIEVING IS AN ACTION

We often think of actions as physical behaviors that can be observed by others (hitting, cursing, cheating, killing, stealing, etc.). But there are actions that are more subtle and may not be observable by others. These subtle actions are seen and recorded by the God of heaven because He knows the heart.

While lust, fantasy, hatred, bitterness, and the like can be actions which are unseen from the human eye, we know we have moved beyond the thought or temptation when we believe and embrace that thought and make it our own. When we are tempted to lust, we are faced with a choice: Do we dismiss the thought and refuse to believe the enemy's lies, or do we embrace the thought and ponder the lies? For example, lust and fantasy are the result of pausing to embrace the passing thought—by relishing in the pleasure of the moment rather than immediately dismissing the thought outright. Another example, bitterness and hatred are the result of refusing [action] to forgive another.

The Apostle Paul says we can be angry and not sin:

Be ye angry, and sin not: let not the sun go down upon your wrath (Eph. 4:26 KJV).

We can be angry and sin, and we can be angry and not sin. It appears, at least on the surface, that when we take the action of letting the sun go down on our anger, we sin. The distinction is in which action we take with regard to our anger. Paul seems to be saying that by letting the sun go down on our anger, we are refusing to let it go. Do we let anger migrate into bitterness and hatred, or do we turn it over to God and let Him deal with the circumstances?

When we believe the enemy's lies, that is just as much an action on our part as believing the truth of Jesus Christ as Lord and Savior. Believing lies puts us into bondage to the enemy. Believing the truth sets us free from that bondage. The lies we believe contractually bind us to the enemy. The truth we believe contractually binds us to the heart of God. Believing is an action and not at all passive.

EVE, A CASE STUDY IN TEMPTATION

Let's take a brief look at the biblical record of Eve in the garden of Eden (Gen. 3:4-6) and her encounter with the enemy who took the form of a serpent:

1. The serpent lied to Eve by saying that God said she could "not eat from any tree in the garden."

2. Eve tries to correct the serpent's misunderstanding that it is only one tree from which they cannot eat.

3. The serpent lies again to Eve: "You will not certainly die."

4. The serpent tells Eve the truth but implies the subtle lie that God is trying to keep something desirable from her: "God knows that when you eat from it your eyes will be opened, and you will be like God, knowing good and evil."

5. Eve's response shows the process by which she ultimately crossed the line to eat the fruit (intent + action):

   · "The woman saw that the fruit of the tree was good for food [desire (intent)],

   · "and pleasing to the eye [desire (intent)],

   · "and also desirable for gaining wisdom [desire (intent)],

   · "she took some and ate it [intent + action = sin (covet)]."

It is at the point of the union of her desire (intent) with her action (eating the fruit) where Eve sins. She coveted gaining wisdom and being like God, and that covetousness resulted in her acquiring the fruit for herself. Her choice to eat the fruit (action) led to Adam also eating of the fruit thereby bringing death and destruction upon the whole earth and humanity.

SUMMARY

We have not been left alone by God to white-knuckle our way through life. God does not want us to be overwhelmed by the seemingly impossible task of ruling over sin. God is in the midst of the battle with us every step of the way.

For since He Himself was tempted in that which He has suffered, He is able to come to the aid of those who are tempted (Heb. 2:18 NASB).

As you consider God's directive to rule over sin, this understanding of the link between the action *(actus reus)*, intent *(mens rea)*, and knowledge may shed significant light on whether or not God is asking you to do the impossible when He directs you to rule over sin and to obey and keep His commands. Moses stated it well:

Now what I am commanding you today is not too difficult for you or beyond your reach (Deut. 30:11).

OBJECTIONS

What about Uzaah who touched the ark and was struck dead by God in II Samuel 6:1-7 and 1 Chronicles 13:9-12? He was apparently trying to steady the cart so it would not tip over and damage the ark.

First of all, the law clearly states that the only ones who were authorized to carry the holy things within the temple were the Kohathites (Num. 4:15). The descendants of Aaron, the Kohanim, had the special role as priests in the Tabernacle in the wilderness and also in the Temple in Jerusalem. They were charged with handling the holy things in the Tabernacle and later the Temple. David brought men (apparently not Levites or Kohathites) with him to collect the ark rather than follow the law and let the Kohathites carry the ark.

Secondly, the ark was to be carried by the Kohathites on their shoulders with poles and not on a cart; using any cart whether new or old was forbidden (Exod. 25:12-14; Num. 7:9).

While one cannot be completely certain, some scholars believe that Abinadab was a Levite and thus familiar with the law (1 Sam. 7:1-2; 1 Chron. 13:7). As a Levite, he knew, or should have known, the law regarding the transporting of the ark from one place to another. In addition, David who repeatedly exclaims that he loves God's law, knew or should have known the law regarding the transporting of the ark.

In spite of the above, the Bible states that Uzzah's act (*actus reus*) was done with an "irreverent" (*mens rea*) intent (II Sam. 6:7 NASB). The God of heaven does not need protection like the pagan idols require. Nor can we be irreverent when we approach God. It appears that Uzzah had lost sight of God and was instead focused on the ark.

The Philistines, who took captive the ark, did not treat the ark in accordance with the Mosaic law. While First Samuel 5 and 6 describe the physical ailments they suffered while they had the ark, there is no evidence that anyone was killed in a similar way to Uzaah when they touched or mishandled the ark while it was in their possession.

We have determined by many examples in scripture that God is always just. While we may not have all the facts in this instance and it may not be obvious that Uzzah had evil intent, one should not automatically assume that God was unjust in this event. God will not remove all doubt for those who choose to doubt. Either God was unjust by punishing Uzzah, or God justly punished him. God will let you doubt Him if that is your desire. When there is room for doubt in one story, one should not build a theological understanding based on partial information. There is room in this passage for a reasonable person to conclude that Uzzah was punished for having both the unlawful action (*actus reus*) and an "irreverent" intent (*mens rea*).

Chapter Eight:

Only by God's Authority

So far, we have established a framework for understanding the implementation of the freedom protocol. Now, let's put wheels on this framework by recognizing the authority God put in place to enforce the contracts we've renounced.

FIGURE 4. **Life weighted down by the enemy's kingdom.**

For years I thought having victory over sin was difficult. Life seemed more heavily weighted toward the enemy's kingdom than God's kingdom. It seemed I was always at a disadvantage; in fact, it was often easier to sin than to resist temptation. It seemed fundamentally unfair that the enemy could lie to me in millions of attractive ways while God is "stuck" with the boring truth.

Many times we feel it is easier to fall toward the enemy's kingdom instead of struggle toward God's kingdom. To live for God in this way is what I call the white-knuckle experience. It's exhausting—so what is the solution? "How can a young person stay on the path of purity? By living according to your word" (Psalm 119:9). As we believe and embrace the truth God reveals according to His word, our life begins to change.

TRUTH SETS YOU FREE

Jesus said, "And ye shall know the truth, and the truth shall make you free" (John 8:32 KJV). This is one of those scriptures that en-

courages us when we read it, but when you ponder the meaning, it
leads to questions like these:

- What is the truth that you need to know to be free?

- Once you discover that truth, from what exactly are you
  set free?

Might knowing what we want to be set free from offer insight
into the essential truth we need to know? Truly, the potential of
this verse is wonderful and limitless. When we know the truth, the
promise is that the truth *will* set us free.

Let's look at this verse in context. When Jesus spoke those words
of freedom, He was speaking to believers who had believed in Him:

*To the Jews who had believed him, Jesus said, "If you hold to my
teaching, you are really my disciples. Then you will know the truth,
and the truth will set you free" (John 8:31-32).*

As believers, the first step to actualizing the promise of His
words is to hold to His teachings; thus, in doing this, Jesus assures
that we will know the truth and the truth will set us free.

Jesus is the truth, and the Holy Spirit leads us to all truth.

I am the way and the truth and the life (John 14:6a).

*But when he, the Spirit of truth, comes, he will guide you into all
the truth (John 16:13a).*

These verses are not limited to theology or doctrine. It appears
that Jesus is referring to the truth about any issue. If the truth is
known, it sets us free from the lies and deceptions of the enemy
and from the resulting contracts. If we apply the principle of John
8:32—*then you will know the truth, and the truth will set you free*—to
the lies we have believed, we should expect that knowing, believing,
and embracing the truth about that issue will free us from the en-

emy's unlimited access to our hearts. Jesus' claim in this verse seems pretty straightforward.

Kingdom Of Darkness (Lies)

Kingdom Of Light (Truth)

FIGURE 5. Life weighted toward God's kingdom.

When we allow life's influences to be more heavily-weighted toward the truth and God's kingdom, we can fully enjoy the life God has in store for us without the white-knuckle experience. One truth from God can instantaneously destroy and nullify millions of lies of the enemy and set us free.

The truth plays out routinely in the lives of people I counsel. Where they were previously harassed, tormented, and overwhelmed by the enemy regarding a specific sin, they become free to experience peace and joy and, with that, find new energy to resist the enemy's lies as they trust in God's authority. They have learned to seek Him, relying on Him through the process and not on themselves. Though they fail at times, they have resolved to deny the enemy access to their lives on a consistent basis; in other words, they become free from the binding contracts of the enemy. Again, it is the truth and only the truth that can set us free from the sin that binds us.

BENEFITS OF FOLLOWING GOD'S DESIGN TO RULE OVER SIN

While it is not possible to immediately overcome *every* sin in our lives, there are six important things that happen when we follow God's design to rule over sin. Let's look at what occurs when we identify the lie, embrace the truth, repent and renounce the lies of the enemy, and ask God to lawfully void the contracts we've made:

1. We are no longer harassed and tormented by the enemy with regard to the renounced sin and voided contract.

2.   God now stands at the door of our hearts to limit the enemy's access to us.

3.   God places parameters on the enemy when He grants him access to us, so that we have a way of escape and will not be overwhelmed.

4.   Our ability to successfully identify, resist, and renounce the enemy's lies and temptations dramatically increases.

5.   Feelings of failure, despair, and havoc no longer have the same intensity.

6.   We experience an immediate peace in our lives.

While temptation is dramatically reduced, there are at least two reasons why God may grant access to the enemy to tempt us in the future: to remind us that we still need Him in our battles with the enemy, and to train us to resist lies and embrace truth, thus strengthening our faith.

WE ARE THE AGENTS. GOD IS THE ENFORCER.

If we stop here, one could get the idea that we, apart from God, are powerful enough to force the enemy to behave himself just by our renouncing his lies and believing the truth.

There are those who believe that because they are God's children, saved by the blood of Jesus, they can command the enemy to do anything, and he will do it. This error has led many into a false sense of their own importance and authority. I have seen people walk around casting out demons with no thought as to whether they are unjustly trespassing on the enemy's property rights or not. God will certainly save all those who call on His name, but it will always be done justly, and not by unjustly trespassing on the enemy's property rights. (See Acts 19:13-16.)

Remember, we are God's agents. We can renounce the enemy's lies and embrace the truth. But who is going to actually void the enemy's contract rights and enforce God's contractual rights in a lawful manner? We can't do that, and I doubt the enemy will listen to our demands if we try to rule over sin in our own strength. Understanding the lawful authority we have in Christ and acting in a just manner means we are cooperating with God when we exercise the remedies[56] He has made available to us in the Bible. By accessing these remedies, God gets all the credit and glory while we receive the benefits. God gives us the authority to lawfully renounce the enemy's contracts, but only God has the power to void them.

While those who are in Christ should live at peace, those who do not believe have no such protection against the enemy:

> *Some Jews who went around driving out evil spirits tried to invoke the name of the Lord Jesus over those who were demon-possessed. They would say, "In the name of the Jesus whom Paul preaches, I command you to come out." Seven sons of Sceva, a Jewish chief priest, were doing this. One day the evil spirit answered them, "Jesus I know, and Paul I know about, but who are you?" Then the man who had the evil spirit jumped on them and overpowered them all. He gave them such a beating that they ran out of the house naked and bleeding (Acts 19:13-16).*

Realistically speaking, there are two ways to rule:

- Have all the guns and the bullets;

- Be an agent of someone who has all the guns and the bullets.

A hundred-pound police officer does not get your attention and obedience because of her stature. She commands your obedience because she represents the full force of the government. If she calls

---

56. Remedies 1 or 2. (See figures 4 and 5 on pages 87 and 89.)

for backup, many more officers will soon show up in full force to protect her and to enforce the law. In the same manner, because I know that God is always perfectly just, I know that He is not afraid or unwilling to protect me or enforce His property rights by instructing the enemy to leave me alone.[57] I can represent God as His agent, but since He is the one who actually makes things happen, I must rely on His justice and trust that He will void the lie-filled contracts I have renounced. There is no authority or power which resides in me that can force the enemy to perform.

DOES GOD EXERCISE HIS PROPERTY RIGHTS?

As stated earlier, contracts are property. When we agree with the enemy, binding contracts with property rights are established. When we agree with God, binding contracts with property rights are also established. Here is a most important question: Will God stand up for and defend His property rights? The answer is a resounding YES.

We must never forget that God is by nature perfectly just. Every act He does must be perfectly just and lawful. God cannot violate principles of His own law (in this case, the enemy's contracted property rights).

Those who have been begging God to take away a problem or addiction are actually asking God—who is not a party to their contract with the enemy—to violate the enemy's property rights. In common law this is called criminal trespass.[58] While it is certain that God wants us to live free of any binding contract with the enemy, asking God to arbitrarily void such a contract is asking Him to commit a criminal trespass on that contract, thus violating principles of law, which are a reflection of His own character.

---

57. Jesus said, "Do you think I cannot call on my Father, and he will at once put at my disposal more than twelve legions of angels?" (Matt. 26:53).

58. In modern law, this is called tortious interference.

Consider this very important principle of law: If you want relief, you must exercise *__THE__* appropriate remedy in a timely manner.

You must exercise *__THE__* remedy not merely *__A__* remedy of your own choosing. An example in United States law explains this point: Congress authorized the selling of credit information by credit reporting agencies to third parties. However, Congress also created *__THE__* remedy for the consumer in the form of an opt-out program.[59] If anyone filed a complaint in court to stop the credit reporting agency from selling their information, it would be dismissed. The court would likely state that you "failed to state a claim upon which relief can be granted." In other words, *__THE__* remedy would not be found in court (at least initially) but, rather, in your actions to use the opt-out program that had been provided for you by Congress. Therefore, if you want relief, you must exercise *__THE__* remedy and not *__A__* remedy of your own choosing.

__THE__ remedy for our sin is Jesus Christ's death on the cross (referred to previously in chapter six as Remedy #1[60]). That sacrifice, when acknowledged and accepted by us, gives us a new position in Christ, and we are saved from the stain and pollution of sin. If we do not start here, everything else we do is merely *__A__* remedy of our own choosing, which will not bring us the desired relief. There is also *__THE__* remedy which delivers us from the power of sin (referred to previously as Remedy #2). Exercising this remedy happens in relationship with Christ and enables us to rule over sin by relying on God's authority to lawfully void the enemy's contracts.

59. *United States, Congress, "CFPB Supervision and Examination Manual." CFPB Supervision and Examination Manual, 2012, pp. FCRA 7-FCRA 7. Version 2.*

60. One could argue that God redeemed and purchased back the world to Himself and that He has the right to exercise His property rights which were established by Jesus Christ on the cross. While this is true, we have the power of choice and are free to contract with the enemy of our souls. When we have truly given our hearts to Jesus, we will want to be delivered from the power of sin and those binding contracts as well.

EVERYONE HAS EQUAL ACCESS TO GOD

For God to be perfectly just when it comes to our ruling over the power of sin, He must level the playing field for all of us, giving everyone equal access to His remedies. Otherwise, resisting sin and obeying God belongs only to the strong and disciplined. What does the Bible teach us about this level playing field?

In the book of Numbers, God instituted cities of refuge.[61] In the event that someone took another person's life by accident, they could flee to a city of refuge for protection until it could be determined if there was foul play or not. There were six cities of refuge scattered throughout Israel.

FIGURE 6. Ancient Israel's cities of refuge.

When God provided this relief through these cities of refuge, He revealed much about the level playing field He applies to His plan of salvation for us:[62]

1. The cities of refuge were scattered throughout Israel, so no one was more than a day's journey from a city of refuge when it was needed.

2. The cities of refuge were on major roads, and the way to each city was clearly marked.

3. The routes to the cities of refuge were main roads, always maintained, never to be impassible, and open year-round to everyone.

---

61. Numbers 35, Joshua 20, and Deuteronomy 19:2.

62. Matthew Henry's *Concise Commentary on the Whole Bible* (Thomas Nelson 2003) for Numbers 35 is a good starting place in studying the cities of refuge.

4. The cities of refuge were to be on a plain and not on a mountain top. If they had been on mountain tops, only the healthy and strong would have been able to obtain relief; access had to be available for the physically challenged as well.

God designed the plan of salvation, which includes both cleansing from the <u>pollution</u> of sin and deliverance from the <u>power</u> of sin. Whether you've been a believer for eighty years or you received Jesus eighty minutes ago, everyone has equal access to the remedies God established for us to rule over sin.

Have you noticed that when we are born into the Kingdom of God, we are not born into a nursery? On the contrary, when we are born again into God's kingdom, we are born in the middle of the battlefield.

It is expected from the first minute of spiritual birth that we immediately engage with the enemy. To do so, we must use all available remedies provided to us by God. As soon as some give their lives to Christ, they have trouble in their family, at work, or in the neighborhood. Sometimes the attacks can feel relentless. Even to a young believer, all the protections, resources, and remedies of heaven are available, just as they are to the spiritually mature believer.

CASE EXAMPLES OF GOD'S POWER OVER OUR SIN

KALINI AND GOD'S SILENT PROTECTION

Several years ago, I was talking with Kalini, who was fifteen years a lesbian, and I referred to the contracts described above as *doors we open* to the enemy: *When we sin, we open a door to the enemy and he can come and go at will because we granted him access.* As I was sharing this concept with her, she said, "I think those doors are already closed." I asked her to explain:

Kalini said, "I went to a social event that had about forty-five people in attendance. Half were straight, and half were gay. Everyone was standing and visiting in what could loosely be described as a semicircle. I was standing at the top of the semicircle so I could see everything going on. I noticed one woman to my right who started touching other women inappropriately as she moved from one end of the semicircle to the other. She moved from woman to woman. As she got closer to me, I wondered what would happen. When she finally got to me, she stood in front of me and just looked at me. There was a pregnant silence. Then, without saying a word, she moved to the woman to my left and picked up where she left off.

"Later I spoke to a friend of mine and told her about what happened. She said, 'You didn't see what I saw. That same woman came up behind you with her hands up like she was going to grab you. Then she stopped, put her hands down, and walked away.'"

I can't tell you exactly what happened there, but if indeed Kalini had been freed from those contracts, which would grant the enemy access to her life, then it appears that God protected Kalini and refused that woman any access to her. I can envision the Holy Spirit whispering to that woman, "Don't you dare touch my property!" This woman was turned away, not just once, but twice.

As you can see, if a new believer or a very mature believer can effectively break and renounce contracts with the enemy, they both can have the same protection from God over their lives. Certainly having God guarding the door of our lives is much better than dealing with the enemy in our own strength. Wouldn't it be better to let God protect His contract property rights—access to our lives—than to struggle with the enemy's relentless attacks every day?[63]

---

63. Unbelievers are either unaware of God's remedies for the pollution of sin and the power of sin, which Jesus won for them on the cross, or, even though they know of these remedies, they choose to reject these benefits provided by God.

KAIPO AND IMMEDIATE FREEDOM

Kaipo had a problem with pornography for more than a decade. He successfully renounced the contracts he had formed with the enemy and returned the access permission back to God. He experienced an amazing freedom. In a few weeks Kaipo called me and said, "I am sure you've experienced this; you innocently begin to think about something and, little by little, you suddenly find yourself thinking impure thoughts. This happened to me and after about five minutes of that kind of thinking, I realized what I was doing. I immediately prayed to renounce those evil thoughts and gave that ground back to God. It was amazing. The enemy left so quickly, I couldn't remember the thoughts I had renounced."

In dealing with the enemy, it is far better and easier for us to let God handle the enemy. We do this by being certain that our contracts are with God and not with the enemy of our souls.

Chapter Nine:

Identifying Lies

Knowing the truth is just as important as knowing the lies. Being equipped with the tools presented in this chapter, we will be able to recognize when we're being presented with a lie and when we've been believing a lie. When lies are identified, it is much easier to apply the truth to effectively renounce the lies and ask God to void the enemy's contracts.

There are two types of lies: circumstantial and foundational. Circumstantial lies are directly related to *current* circumstances, and foundational lies are directly related to *past* lies we may have believed for many years, even decades.

CIRCUMSTANTIAL LIES

When Furnell and Martha sat down to one of their final sessions, I asked them how things were going. Martha said things had been going really well except for one moment where she had a bit of a problem. I asked her what happened:

"Furnell and I were driving along one evening when I asked him a question. He responded, but I didn't like his answer. I got a little testy with him and snapped back."

"So there was conflict, right?" I said.

"Yes."

"What was the lie you were believing that led to the conflict?" I said.

"I don't know.[64] I just thought Furnell was trying to aggravate me."

"Yes, the enemy whispered to you that Furnell was trying to aggravate you." I continued, "If you didn't know if Furnell was trying to aggravate you or not, how would you find out if that thought was the truth or a lie?"

"I am not sure," she said.

"What if you were to ask Furnell *Are you trying to aggravate me?*" I suggested.

"I did ask him."

"Oh. And what did he say?" I said—but this time looked right at Furnell.

"No, I am not trying to aggravate you," Furnell said, still showing the same look of surprise he must have shown Martha that same night.

"Martha, let's recap," I said. "The enemy whispered to you that Furnell was trying to aggravate you, and Furnell told you he wasn't. It seems that you did not believe Furnell and chose instead to believe the enemy and his lie. The result was conflict."

In this circumstance, the lie was <u>Furnell is trying to aggravate Martha</u>. The truth was <u>Furnell was not trying to aggravate Martha</u>. When Martha believed the lie—confusion and conflict resulted. When she renounced the lie and believed the truth, peace and harmony resulted. She immediately looked at Furnell and gave him one of the best apologies ever.

---

64. Often when I ask a client what the lie is, they immediately say, "I don't know," and then immediately follow that statement with the lie they believed.

Did you notice that Martha did not go through a formal process of renouncing the lie? She believed and embraced the truth and renounced the lie in a moment. Understanding the lie is helpful in that it can clarify and deepen our understanding of the truth. However, it is the truth and only the truth, when believed and embraced, that sets you free.

FOUNDATIONAL LIES

Foundational lies can be a bit tricky. This is true because they often do not have anything to do with the immediate circumstance or issue at hand. They seem to be lurking in the shadows, close enough to affect us, but staying far enough out of sight to be unnoticed.

Freddie and Linda had a rocky marriage. It was great for the first few years, but then Freddie began to snap back at Linda even if what she said was benign.

One evening after Freddie disciplined their children, Linda suggested he could've spoken a bit kinder while disciplining them. Freddie flew off the handle and yelled at Linda: "I never have your support in discipline. I am doing my best to help our kids become responsible adults, and all I get from you is criticism."

Both agreed later that Linda was pretty reasonable in the way she had approached Freddie about his lack of kindness. What was the problem and why was Freddie so snarky with Linda?

After hearing Freddie's life story, it became clear that he grew up constantly hearing the lie *you can't do anything right*. Over time, he grew to believe it, which began to affect his own responses to others when they touched that pain in his heart.

It's possible that Freddie heard that lie only once or twice in his entire childhood; nonetheless, his thinking had been formed by the lie he believed. A child rarely questions the truth of an authority figure's statements; what they say must be true, so Freddie accepted that lie as the truth.

When he recognized this foundational lie, he renounced it and embraced the truth: *you do many things right*. Thereafter, he was able to accept his wife's comments and suggestions without that same pain shooting through his heart each time. He found himself less offended by others and able to respond in a more loving and positive way. He even took the next step and resolved bitterness and resentment he had been holding—by forgiving the ones who told him those lies many years earlier.

FOOTPRINTS

Everywhere Jesus and the enemy go they leave footprints. Just as a good tracker can tell much about an animal by looking at its footprints, we can discern who has been walking through our hearts by the footprints that remain.

THE ENEMY'S FOOTPRINTS

The enemy's footprints are distinctive: lies, fear, doubt, chaos, confusion, conflict, isolation, and accusation to name a few. These evidences not only apply to spiritual matters or Christian theology, but to every circumstance of life. If we are in the middle of a business negotiation and the enemy's footprints are evident, his influence is there. It may be circumstantial or foundational. If you are a tall man negoti-

FIGURE 7.
The enemy's footprint.

ating with a short man who believes that all tall people are dishonest and do not respect short people, even that lie can cause problems during the negotiating process.

JESUS' FOOTPRINTS

FIGURE 8.
Jesus' footprint

Jesus administers His kingdom through the Holy Spirit, and it's the Holy Spirit's job to lead us into all truth.

But when he, the Spirit of truth, comes, he will guide you into all the truth. He will not speak on his own; he will speak only what he hears, and he will tell you what is yet to come (John 16:13).

When we embrace this biblical truth, we become filled with the fruit of the Spirit (Gal. 5:22-23). Jesus' footprints are distinctive: love, joy, peace, forbearance, kindness, goodness, faithfulness, gentleness, and self-control. Each of these spiritual fruits apply to every circumstance of life, even the secular, or non-spiritual, parts of our lives, and they will ultimately lead to community and relationships.

RECOGNIZING THE FOOTPRINTS

Mike and Gladys had been working hard on their relationship to resolve issues that had been tripping them up for years. One morning at the breakfast table, they got into a discussion that started out okay but soon began to break down into conflict and chaos. In that moment Gladys looked over to Mike and said, "Whose footprints are we seeing here?" They both paused, looked at each other, realized and embraced the truth of what was going on, and immediately experienced peace. They did not even resolve the issue at that moment, but by pausing and reflecting on the footprints, they could easily see who was influencing their conversation. The enemy was stopped dead in his tracks.

Often there are times and circumstances when it's more appropriate to resolve the offending issues at a later time. Mike and

Gladys chose to do that. And when they address that issue later, they will be watching for footprints to determine who is influencing their discussion.

RECOGNIZING THE EXTREMES

The enemy is tricky and deceptive and opposes God at every turn, constantly lying to undo or destroy the truth that God is speaking into our lives. One tactic is to push you from one extreme to the other or from one lie to another.

When you are looking for the truth, be careful not to go to the opposite extreme only later to find yourself believing another lie or, worse yet, believing the truth wrapped in a lie. Pursue the truth guided by the word of God until you find the peace He desires you to have.

RELATIONSHIP VS. ISOLATION

Another difference between the footprints of Jesus and the footprints of the enemy is that while the truth God speaks to our hearts will always lead us into relationship and association with Him and others, the enemy and his lies lead us into isolation.

For instance, a person can be isolated when they go to a party, even though they're surrounded by people. Everyone knows what it is like to feel alone in a crowded room. The presence of people does not necessarily counteract one's feeling of isolation.

A temptation for some is seeking sex or drugs at a party. Consider the motive needed to go to this party: How much fun can **I** have? Who can help **me** have more fun? The enemy's temptations tend to isolate us from meaningful community and relationships. At this party, how many people are building loving and caring relationships? Isn't everyone out to satisfy their own self-centered pleasure?

Often, the goal of the attenders, whether they know it or not, is to get temporary relief and pleasure for themselves. They are exchanging *real* relationship-based joy for self-centered pleasure.

Think of all the things commonly described as sin, and you will find that each one leads *away* from community and relationship with God and others. Pornography does not help you get closer to your wife. Drug and alcohol abuse does not help families become closer. Bitterness does not help us enjoy healthy relationships and fellowship. I challenge you to find one temptation (lie) of the enemy that does not ultimately lead to both isolation and disassociation from others and from God.

God, on the other hand, is all about relationships and community. Everything He offers us in this life is focused on developing richer, more satisfying relationships with Him and others. Those who get free of pornography, drug, and alcohol addictions are better able to connect with loved ones at the heart level. They find themselves able to care about others' emotional needs as well as their own. Those who get free from bitterness become interested in community, such as church, and reconnecting with the people who wounded them so deeply. They begin to realize that offenders are deeply wounded themselves and in need of love and understanding. When someone strikes out against you again, is your first thought about how you have been wounded, or is it about how wounded and broken they are? If you can see only your pain, it's very likely you've picked up bitterness again. It's time to forgive.

These footprint indicators of relationship and isolation are our signs. Be ruthlessly honest with yourself as you make evaluations of whose footprints you're tracking. Look at long-term evidence rather than short-term. While you may think that committing adultery might bring you closer to that other man or woman who seems to really care about you, in the long run, it will destroy not only your marriage and your relationship with your children, but with many other family members, friends, and God as well. Lies and sin lead to isolation.

> *Whoever isolates himself seeks his own desire; he breaks out against all sound judgment (Prov. 18:1 English Standard Version, ESV).*

Real joy and peace can only be found in the midst of relationship with God and others.

> *And let us consider how we may spur one another on toward love and good deeds, not giving up meeting together, as some are in the habit of doing, but encouraging one another—and all the more as you see the Day approaching (Heb. 10:24-25).*

> *But when he, the Spirit of truth, comes, he will guide you into all the truth (John 16:13a).*

LOOK BEYOND THE ACTIONS

We tend to focus almost entirely on actions:

- The adultery, not the lies that convinced me that I had married the wrong woman;

- The murder, not the lies that said I would have justice if they were dead;

- The robbery, not the lies that made me believe I deserve to have more;

- The outburst of anger, not the lies that said I could control someone with my words;

- The cursing, not the lies that said cursing makes me look cool and tough; or

- The violence, not the lies that seduced me into thinking I can violate another's person.

Whether it is our own actions or those of others, we spend most of our lives focused on the outcome of the lies we believe and not the lies themselves. Doesn't it feel at times that Christians spend much of their time putting Band-Aids on the symptoms rather than performing surgery on the infection? When we focus on actions and not on the lies which led to those actions, the offender will seldom find freedom to behave differently.

The enemy is a master at getting us to focus on actions. Review the last argument you had with someone. Most likely it was about an action someone did or words someone said or didn't say. We get so wrapped up in the argument, we fail to notice the footprints, whether circumstantial or foundational. If in these moments, we'd stop to ask each other what lies we are believing, real problems would be addressed and lasting solutions would rise to the surface. Agree with each other to be willing to take a hard look at the lies when they arise. Be intentional and plan ahead to cooperate and get to the bottom of what the heart is feeling. Once the heart issue related to any argument is resolved, it is nearly impossible to go back and pick up the old argument again. This is because what you thought the argument was about was not the issue at all. Someone's heart was wounded, and at the root of that wound was a lie of the enemy. When you get to the bottom of that lie, hearts get cared for and most arguments simply evaporate.

As a church, we should be committed to marching through the gates of hell to rescue wounded souls who have been lied to and bound by the enemy for decades. In doing so, we must look beyond their actions.

WHAT IS REPENTANCE?

The Greek and Hebrew meaning for repentance means "to change one's mind" or "a change of mind." We generally think of repentance as being associated with sorrow and tears. While sorrow can be a part of repentance, that is not the meaning of the word as used in scripture. When Peter preached his gospel sermon on the Day of Pentecost, he used the word *repent*. Here is Peter's interaction with the crowd on the Day of Pentecost:

> *"Therefore let all Israel be assured of this: God has made this Jesus, whom you crucified, both Lord and Messiah." When the people heard this, they were cut to the heart and said to Peter and the other apostles, "Brothers, what shall we do?" Peter replied, "Repent [change your mind about Jesus] and be baptized, every one of you, in the name of Jesus Christ for the forgiveness of your sins. And you will receive the gift of the Holy Spirit. The promise is for you and your children and for all who are far off—for all whom the Lord our God will call (Acts 2:36-39).*

This understanding of the word *repent* or *repentance* helps us to transition from the enemy's lies to God's truth. To put it simply, we must choose to change our minds regarding the lie, and then choose to believe and embrace the truth. This process of choosing to let our minds come into conformity with the truth as revealed by God is called *sanctification*. It is a work in the hearts and minds of those who have started the journey with God to restore their thinking back to Godly thinking, which is based in truth.

> *Sanctify them through thy truth: thy word is truth (John 17:17 KJV).*

Some have told me they question their conversion because they did not have the sorrow and tears they thought should accompany repentance and true conversion. This should not be of concern because we are all different and therefore experience God in various ways. But in every case, no matter what level of emotion we have at the time of our conversion, there is a definite change of mind to conform to God's thinking. This is how Paul explains it:

Don't copy the behavior and customs of this world, but let God transform you into a new person by <u>changing the way you think</u>. Then you will learn to know God's will for you, which is good and pleasing and perfect (Rom. 12:2 New Living Translation, NLT; emphasis mine).

IS IT NECESSARY TO KNOW THE LIE?

The short answer is NO. One might be able to achieve some level of freedom by embracing the truth without understanding the lies. So why the emphasis on identifying the lies?

If I have a clear understanding of my sinful life and the depths of darkness to which I have descended and from which I have been saved, God's grace is very precious to me and the contrast is profound. However, if my opinion is that I am generally a good person, then even though I might accept God's grace, the power of that grace in my life is not as effective. In my mind there will be little contrast between my life without God's grace and my life with God's grace. In other words, the greater the contrast between my sin and God's grace, the more wonderful that grace is to me personally, and the more powerful it will be in bringing about change in my life.

Consider for a moment God's mercy and grace: Jesus took our punishment (death) for sin upon Himself, which we deserve, and offers us the blessing of eternal life, which we do not deserve. While we might be obedient to God at times, our lives as a whole do not merit His grace, mercy, and blessing. For example, if I am disqualified two feet from the starting line in the Boston Marathon, does it help me if I finish the race an hour ahead of everyone else? Being obedient from now on does not address my past disobedience and sin for which justice demands satisfaction. We are indeed blessed by God for our obedience to Him, but that blessing always remains undeserved when contrasted with the totality of our life.

The more clearly we understand the enemy's lies, the more wonderful truth is to us. Understanding truth alone, without understanding the lies and their consequences, can rob us of the full impact of grace, of which we are in desperate need. We do not want temporary relief; we want long-term and long-lasting results—healing.

Finally, we often want to pick the truth we wish to believe and avoid those truths we don't want to believe or are too difficult to accept. We may be asking God to reveal the lies to us in one area of our life and yet, we have refused to repent of other lies that God has previously revealed to us in *other* areas of our life. To operate in this manner is to worship and serve God on our terms, not His. True breakthrough happens when we follow the leading of the Holy Spirit. Though a particular truth presented might be the most difficult from which to repent, it will likely help us see the other lies more clearly and will significantly accelerate our advancement toward freedom and the abundant life God has for us.

When you are experiencing chaos, confusion, and conflict, the first question you should always ask is, "God, what is the lie I am believing?" When He reveals the lie(s) to you, immediately repent of that lie, renounce it and replace it with the truth He has revealed to you, no matter how difficult it may seem. Then ask Him to protect your heart and the contract you have with Him (His property rights). This is worshiping, loving, and serving God on His terms.

For though we walk in the flesh, we do not war according to the flesh, for the weapons of our warfare are not of the flesh, but divinely powerful for the destruction of fortresses. We are destroying speculations and every lofty thing raised up against the knowledge of God, and we are taking every thought captive to the obedience of Christ (II Cor. 10:3-5 NASB).

Chapter Ten:

Forgiveness

The difficulty we have with forgiving others stems from our deep-seated desire for justice. This should be no surprise; after all, we were created in God's image and He is perfectly just. We are wired to desire justice. The problem is we want it right now and, often, we want to personally impose the punishment, wanting that person to justly pay for the pain and consequences their actions have caused. Our battle when it comes to forgiveness is often not with the small offenses but rather, the offenses that have deeply wounded us.

As we interact with each other, we oftentimes find that we have wounded someone. When that happens, we "owe" that person an apology. Let's refer to this as a debt we owe. There are some debts we can easily pay and some debts that are impossible to pay. If I steal your lawnmower, I can buy you another one, but if I were to kill your child, I could never repay that debt. I could not do anything that would bring satisfaction or peace to your heart. Clearly some wounds result in debts that are impossible to pay.

In the gospel of Matthew, Jesus tells the parable of the unjust servant:

"Therefore the kingdom of heaven is like a certain king who wanted to settle accounts with his servants. And when he had begun to settle accounts, one was brought to him who owed him ten thousand

talents.[65] But as he was not able to pay, his master commanded that he be sold, with his wife and children and all that he had, and that payment be made" (Matt. 18:23-25 New King James Version, NKJV).

The servant was in an impossible situation. The debt he owed was impossible to pay:

"The servant therefore fell down before him, saying, 'Master, have patience with me, and I will pay you all'" (Matt. 18:26 NKJV)—let's call this Plan A.

"Then the master of that servant was moved with compassion, released him, and forgave him the debt" (Matt. 18:26-27 NKJV)—let's call this Plan B.

In other words, Plan A means "the debt must be paid and I will pay the debt"; Plan B means "the debt is forgiven and I no longer owe the debt." Which plan did the servant choose?

"But that servant went out and found one of his fellow servants who owed him a hundred denarii[66]; and he laid hands on him and took him by the throat, saying, 'Pay me what you owe!' So his fellow servant fell down at his feet and begged him, saying, 'Have patience with me, and I will pay you all.' And he would not, but went and threw him into prison till he should pay the debt" (Matt. 18:28-30 NKJV).

Why did the servant grab his fellow servant by the throat and demand a hundred denarii from him? Jesus showed that even though

65. One talent was worth about twenty years of a day laborer's wages. Ten-thousand talents amounted to two-hundred years' worth of wages; a debt which was impossible to pay.

66. A denarius was the usual daily wage of a day laborer. One hundred denarii amounts to about four-months' wages; a debt which is possible to pay.

the servant could never pay back the debt, he chose to implement Plan A (the debt must be paid and I will pay it) instead of Plan B (the debt is forgiven and I no longer owe the debt).

If you have adopted Plan A, then every denarius counts because you are trying to pay back a huge (impossible) debt. If you have adopted Plan B, rather than accost your fellow servant and demand money, you might invite him over to a "debt discharge" party at your house to celebrate the kindness and mercy of your master.

> *"So when his fellow servants saw what had been done, they were very grieved, and came and told their master all that had been done. Then his master, after he had called him, said to him, 'You wicked servant! I forgave you all that debt because you begged me. Should you not also have had compassion on your fellow servant, just as I had pity on you?' And his master was angry, and delivered him to the torturers until he should pay all that was due to him. So My heavenly Father also will do to you if each of you, from his heart, does not forgive his brother his trespasses" (Matt. 18:31-35 NKJV).*

Jesus seems to be saying that we cannot adopt Plan B (debt cancelled) for ourselves and then administer Plan A (debt owed) to others. God says that as we have received His infinite grace and forgiveness for all our debt to Him, so we are to offer that same grace and forgiveness to others.

The choices, then, are these:

1. Trust God and forgive, letting Him obtain the justice you deserve in His time; or

2. Trust no one and don't forgive, personally demanding payment from those who have wounded you.

Demanding justice and refusing to forgive leaves a "black hole" in our hearts that can never be filled or satisfied. By refusing to forgive we will have wasted our lives looking for satisfaction in pursuance of justice, only to find we have become imprisoned by the pain and consequences of how others have wounded us. This is not a life of freedom. Conversely, trusting God to obtain justice for us will ultimately result in justice acquired. Here's how: Jesus already bore their punishment by His sacrifice on the cross just as He bore our debt. Isn't this justice acquired? If the offender does not accept Jesus' payment for their debt, justice will be acquired for their wickedness at the end of time. If we choose to surrender a debt owed us to God and trust that He will obtain justice for us, we can forgive others and be completely free of bitterness. A heart filled with peace will evidence a bitterness-free heart. We are then able to love the offender and care about their brokenness, even if they offend again.

EXAMPLES OF UNFORGIVENESS THAT LED TO BITTERNESS

When we find ourselves bitter or resentful about anything or anyone, someone needs to be forgiven. One of the most destructive contracts we can form with the enemy is choosing unforgiveness, granting him a stronghold of bitterness in our hearts. Here are some examples.

OLIVIA

Olivia wouldn't forgive her husband of his affair, and bitterness had taken a deep place in her heart. When she and her husband, George, came to me for counseling, we began talking about identifying the lies and truth. During the early part of our sessions, Olivia said, "But my husband's affair IS the truth."

I agreed with her that it was the truth but also explained that what was binding her heart in unforgiveness and bitterness were the <u>lies</u> she had believed <u>about the truth</u> of George's affair. Here are some of the lies she had believed for decades:

- Adultery is unforgivable.

- A man can be forgiven any sin but adultery.

- He will do it again.

- I just can't trust any man.

- I can't and won't forgive him until he is truly sorry and repents.

- To forgive my husband means what he did is okay.

She was particularly struggling with the lie that to forgive her husband meant what he did was okay.

"Was what you did okay?" Olivia said to George during a counseling session.

"Absolutely not," George replied.

The source of her confusion and unforgiveness were lies *about the truth*. In believing them, Olivia had formed a contract with the enemy that granted him unfettered access to her heart. This agreement resulted in unforgiveness that turned into bitterness. And it wasn't just toward her husband. After developing an inventory of those who had wounded her, she realized she'd been bitter for decades. She then forgave each person and renounced the bitterness and lies she had believed. She became free of bitterness.

ABIGAIL

I counseled Abigail, who also made a complete inventory of those who had wounded her, but in going through the process of forgiveness, she found one person she could not forgive.

"I can forgive everyone else—except my daughter-in-law," she said.

We spent a long time discussing this issue. I finally asked, "What if we were to cut off your daughter-in-law's legs? Would that help you forgive her? What if we were to ask Jesus to get back on the cross, and then nail His hands and feet to it—again. Would that help?"

In that moment, as Abigail imagined Jesus getting back on the cross to die all over again—she chose to forgive her daughter-in-law.

As we prayed, Abigail said she saw Jesus leaning over and weeping for her daughter-in-law. She had no idea that the pain she felt was breaking Jesus' heart as well. In fact, months later she told me whenever she starts to feel bitter towards her daughter-in-law, she remembers Jesus weeping over her and the bitterness disappears.

EMMA

From the age of eight, Emma was like the mother in the home, preparing meals, cleaning the house, and looking after her siblings. Her mother was an alcoholic.

One night when Emma was eleven, she was awakened by her father: "There is something wrong with your mother." Emma got up and found her mother cold and in rigor mortis—she had committed suicide. Six months later Emma's father remarried. The relationship with her new stepmother was very strained until Emma moved out at seventeen. She eventually got married, had a child, and a happy marriage.

One day, Emma and her family went to Europe with her father and stepmother to visit her father's birthplace. In the seven-seater van they were driving, her stepmother fell asleep at the wheel and drove head-on into another vehicle. Emma believes that she was thrown forward, hitting the base of her husband's skull with her forehead. Everyone survived except Emma's husband. He was taken to the hospital brain-dead, only to be kept alive by machines.

Emma was faced with a horrible decision. In that critical moment, her father was absent from the hospital and she felt abandoned. While on the phone with a neurologist from her home church in the United States, the doctor talked her through the decision to pull the plug. She then had to make the arrangements to get her husband's body back home. Again, her father was not around to help her with this difficult task.

When she processed through her bitterness inventory during our counseling session, the first three people on her list were her mother, father, and stepmother. Forgiving them was excruciating. It took some time to complete her prayer for just these three people. At one point, the enemy lied to her and said *You can't do this*. I assured her that she could get through it, and she proceeded. Upon finishing her prayer of forgiveness for the first three names, she said she already felt better. She forgave the other people on her list as well and was set free from bitterness that day.

A few days later Emma came back for our next session. The first thing she said was "It's amazing."

"What's amazing?" I asked.

"Ordinarily," she said, "when my stepmom calls, I start yelling at everyone and no one can do anything right. It's even worse when she comes over to the house. But when she called last week, it did not affect me. As a matter of fact, when she came over to the house, it didn't affect me at all."

About a year later, I asked Emma how things were going with her stepmom, and she said *Great!* By the way, her stepmother hasn't changed. It's Emma's heart that was changed and set free.

I find that those who have chosen to forgive and have been set free from bitterness in this way remain free even years later. They may have brief temptations to relapse but once they realize what is happening, they have the tools to get back on track and maintain their freedom. We shouldn't be surprised. Jesus said,

"If the Son therefore shall make you free, ye shall be free indeed" *(John 8:36 KJV).*

Observe how God forgives:

"I have given you an example, that you also should do just as I have done to you. Truly, truly, I say to you, a servant is not greater than his master, nor is a messenger greater than the one who sent him" *(John 13:15-16 ESV).*

GIVING AND RECEIVING FORGIVENESS

There are times when someone asks us to forgive them for their actions. There are also times when we are asking others to forgive us for our actions. To get a deeper understanding of forgiveness, let's first look at how we receive forgiveness for our actions.

RECEIVING FORGIVENESS—HOW TO APOLOGIZE

When we apologize, we generally apologize for our actions. If I humiliate Henry in front of a hundred people and later regret what I said, I would call Henry and say, "Henry, I am really sorry about what I said. Will you forgive me?"

Henry will likely say, "Yes, I forgive you." But my apology failed to address a very important issue. I failed to address the way I wounded Henry by what I said. There are fundamental truths with regard to making an apology:

- When we *apologize* for our *actions*, the pain we caused can remain.

- When we *apologize* for the *pain* we caused, we are automatically forgiven for both the *action* and the *pain* we caused.

Most of our apologies are focused on our *actions* and not the *pain* we actually caused, how we broke someone's heart. An effective apology would be "Henry, I was wrong in what I said to you. That must have made you feel humiliated. I am so sorry for the way I humiliated you (wounded you). Would you choose to forgive me?" Apologizing for the pain helps Henry focus on forgiving the pain and not just my actions. By asking Henry to forgive me for the pain, if he forgives me for the pain, my actions will be forgiven as well.

Have you apologized to someone and later, under a similar circumstance, had them bring up that past experience again? Many times, these numerous, incessant reminders are a disguise for what's really going on in the heart. They may have previously forgiven the action intellectually, but the pain still resides in their heart. This is why they may repeatedly bring up the past. They are hoping that you will care for the lingering pain they are still feeling. Many misread this and think people just won't give up on the issue. The real issue is that either you did not ask to be forgiven for the pain you caused or they have not forgiven you for the pain they experienced.

The next time you apologize to someone, find out how it made them feel first. Then ask them to forgive you for that specific pain you caused, and watch what happens. You'll be surprised and pleased at the response you get.

GIVING FORGIVENESS—THE FLIPSIDE OF AN APOLOGY

Giving forgiveness works the same way as receiving forgiveness. There are fundamental truths with regard to forgiving others:

- When we *forgive* another for their *actions*, the pain they caused can remain.

- When we *forgive* another for the *pain* they caused, they are automatically forgiven for both the *action* and the *pain*.

If you were beaten by your father when you were a child then later, you discovered that he had been beaten by his father when he was a child, you now have an understanding of why you were beaten. This new understanding can lead you to think you have forgiven your father. This is what I call "intellectual forgiveness," which is only a better understanding but not forgiveness. If we settle for intellectual forgiveness, we can be fooled by the enemy into thinking we have forgiven and yet remain bound by bitterness.

Although your father's childhood has given you an intellectual understanding of why you were beaten, it does not address your heart. You have been waiting decades for your father to say, "Son, I was wrong when I hit you so severely when you were a child. I treated you unfairly. I caused you to feel fear, and I am deeply sorry for wounding you that way. Would you forgive me?" This is what we long for. When someone apologizes for the pain they caused, it is much easier to connect with and forgive them. This is what Jesus refers to as forgiving from the heart, forgiving someone for the pain they caused you.

> "In anger his master handed him over to the jailers to be tortured, until he should pay back all he owed. This is how my heavenly Father will treat each of you unless you forgive your brother or sister from your heart" (Matt. 18:34-35; emphasis mine).

Understanding Jesus' meaning of forgiveness is a pivotal and foundational point when it comes to forgiving others. If this is not understood, believed, and practiced, we can remain stuck in our unforgiveness and bitterness (the pain and consequences of the offender's actions) for the rest of our lives. The more specifically we identify the pain, the more effective and heart-centered is the forgiveness, and the more free of bitterness we will be.

THE ENEMY'S LIES ABOUT FORGIVENESS

Here are some of the lies many have found themselves believing about forgiveness over the years:

- I can forgive other people, but I cannot forgive *that* person.
- That person's actions are too horrible to forgive.
- Forgiving means that I have to say I am okay with their actions, and I just can't.
- God is not asking me to forgive that person.
- God only forgives those people who confess their sin and repent.
- Some sins are not forgivable.
- They keep reoffending. When they stop, I will forgive them.
- They are not sorry for what they did to me.
- If that person asked me to forgive him, I would.

All of us have been wounded by people, sometimes significantly, by varying degrees and in various ways: emotional, physical, sexual, mental, verbal, or spiritual. Couples in their seventies have come to me for counseling who have been bitter their entire lives over things done to them when they were children. Many have told me they have asked God to take away their bitterness every day, but with no results—and many are bitter at God for not taking it away. This is a good place to reiterate that God will never act unjustly. He is not a taker when it comes to the choices we've made. He won't violate (trespass on) the agreements, or contracts, we have created with the enemy.

FORGIVENESS IS A ONE-WAY STREET

I am sure this may sound odd, but the next hurdle we must overcome is the fact that the pathway to forgiveness is a one-way street.

Forgiveness does not depend on the offending person. Whether the offending party even cares about our forgiveness or not, God requires us to forgive. Our offender may not even remember the offense or may have died since the offense took place. If our freedom from bitterness was dependent upon those who have wounded us, we would be stuck in our bitterness for the rest of our lives. While these situations can make it difficult for us to forgive, Jesus asks us to forgive from the heart regardless.

Are we forgiven by God only after we ask for forgiveness and repent in sorrow? Take a hard look at the following pertinent scriptures. The singular act of Christ's death on the cross shows that God *leads* with forgiveness before we even want it. We then are asked to respond to the forgiveness already in place.

> *But God demonstrates his own love for us in this: <u>While we were still sinners,</u> Christ died for us (Rom. 5:8; emphasis mine).*

> *For if, while we were God's enemies, we were reconciled to him through the death of his Son, how much more, <u>having been reconciled</u> [past tense], shall we be saved through his life! (Rom. 5:10; emphasis mine).*

> *All this is from God, who reconciled us [past tense] to himself through Christ and gave us the ministry of reconciliation: That God was reconciling the world to himself in Christ, not counting people's sins against them. . . . We implore you on Christ's behalf: Be reconciled to God (II Cor. 5:18-20; emphasis mine).*

God reconciled us to Himself, while we were still sinners and while we did not even care. Paul makes his appeal of reconciliation:

> *We pray you in Christ's stead, <u>be ye reconciled</u> to God (II Cor. 5:20; emphasis mine).*

There is nothing in God's heart to obstruct our access to Him. The path to His heart is completely open.

What's most important to understand is that God does not ask us to do what He is unwilling to do. God leads by example.

Be kind and compassionate to one another, forgiving each other, just as in Christ God forgave you (Eph. 4:32).

If we follow God's example, then we are to forgive apart from the other person's attitude about their offense toward us. God has forgiven all, even those who will never care for His forgiveness.

FORGIVENESS IS A DECISION

Forgiveness is a very emotional experience, but it is not a feeling. Forgiveness is a decision. It is a choice that must be made prior to any victory and freedom over bitterness. This means that even if we do not feel like forgiving, we choose to forgive anyway.

When people in my office are in the actual process of forgiving others, they often use phrases like these:

- Lord, I want to forgive.
- Lord, I hope I can forgive.
- Lord, I will forgive.
- Lord, I already forgave.
- Lord, I can forgive.

None of the above phrases constitute a forgiveness from the heart. People find it much easier to use these phrases than to just say, "Lord, I choose to forgive." Tentative forgiveness reflects no commitment or finality. But once they choose to forgive with commitment, at that moment, tears often begin to flow. This is one indication that their heart is in the forgiveness, and it's not just a mental or intellectual exercise.

WILLING TO RELEASE THE DEBT TO GOD

When dealing with the offenses of others, we must follow God's example.

Forgive each other, just as God in Christ also has forgiven you (Eph. 4:32b NASB).

We can be willing to suffer for the pain others have caused us, and in so doing we actually participate in the sufferings of Christ.

Dear friends, do not be surprised at the fiery ordeal that has come on you to test you, as though something strange were happening to you. But rejoice inasmuch as you participate in the sufferings of Christ, so that you may be overjoyed when his glory is revealed (I Pet. 4:12-13).

But whatever gain I had, I counted as loss for the sake of Christ. Indeed, I count everything as loss because of the surpassing worth of knowing Christ Jesus my Lord. For his sake I have suffered the loss of all things and count them as rubbish, in order that I may gain Christ (Phil. 3:7-8 ESV).

Fixing our eyes on Jesus, the pioneer and perfecter of faith. For the joy set before him he endured the cross, scorning its shame, and sat down at the right hand of the throne of God (Heb. 12:2).

When Jesus gave His life on the cross for us, He endured our shame, pain, and suffering because of the joy set before Him—that we would be saved by His sacrifice and suffering.

Not only that, but we rejoice in our sufferings, knowing that suffering produces endurance, and endurance produces character, and character produces hope, and hope does not put us to shame, because God's love has been poured into our hearts through the Holy Spirit who has been given to us (Rom. 5:3-5 ESV).

When we read of the horrible things done to the apostles and prophets of old, didn't they struggle emotionally with what was done to them? Was unforgiveness and bitterness a temptation for them? Was it easier for them to endure the abuse at the hands of others without bitterness than it is for us? We need to be careful not to miss the deep emotional pain they endured. Their response can be our experience as well. Let's take a closer look at this.

Jesus tells us to rejoice when we are persecuted.

Rejoice and be glad, for your reward in heaven is great; for in the same way they persecuted the prophets who were before you (Matt. 5:12 NASB).

Suffering in scripture is not to be a source of bitterness but a reason to rejoice. The disciples could say that they rejoiced to be considered worthy to suffer for the name of Christ.

So they went on their way from the presence of the Council, rejoicing that they had been considered worthy to suffer shame for His name (Acts 5:41 NASB).

The difficulty we have is that we have adopted the world's view of suffering. If we suffer in any way physically, we immediately take a pill to stop the pain. While this can be acceptable at times physically, it puts us in a frame of mind that can bleed over into our spiritual lives.

Humble yourselves, therefore, under God's mighty hand, that he may lift you up in due time. Cast all your anxiety on him because he cares for you (I Pet. 5:6-7).

That is why, for Christ's sake, I <u>delight</u> in weaknesses, in insults, in hardships, in persecutions, in difficulties. For when I am weak, then I am strong (II Cor. 12:10; emphasis mine).

Paul delights in insults and persecutions instead of getting bitter. He rejoices that he is considered worthy to share in Christ's sufferings, a spiritual truth that can only be spiritually discerned. God's kingdom is not like this world.

Paul says that when he is weak then he is strong. Thus, the weaker we discover ourselves to be, the more we must rely on God's remedies to rule over sin. As we rule over sin by God's authority, He brings all the needed guns and bullets to each situation in which we find ourselves.

Praise be to the God and Father of our Lord Jesus Christ, the Father of compassion and the God of all comfort, who comforts us in all our troubles, so that we can comfort those in any trouble with the comfort we ourselves receive from God (II Cor. 1:3-4).

Notice Paul does not say that we are to comfort each other with stories of abuse and pain that are worse than others have experienced. We are to comfort each other with the "comfort" God has given us in all our circumstances. The question is how can we adopt the attitude of the early disciples so that we can rejoice that we are counted worthy to share in Christ's suffering?

An effective way to do this is to be willing to pay for the emotional pain and consequences of what the offender did. We really can't pay for the pain and consequences like Jesus did, but we can rejoice that we are counted worthy to share in Jesus' suffering. If we are NOT *willing* to pay for the emotional pain and consequences of the offender, then *we* will pay and carry the emotional pain and consequences of their actions for the rest of our lives. On the other hand, if we ARE *willing* to embrace and pay for the emotional pain and consequences they have caused us by their actions, then the pain evaporates. We still remember the events and what happened, but the pain is gone.

When someone owes us an apology—there is a debt they owe us. When I am willing to pay for the emotional pain and consequences they caused, it can be "Paid in Full." This is exactly what Jesus did for us on the cross; our sins were "Paid in Full." Jesus asks us to do for others what He did for us.

In this world, bitterness is an accepted way of life. It's at times worn as a badge of discernment. We believe we are expected to live with the pain and consequences of others' actions. Sometimes we feel that it is even God's will, and that it is a burden He's asked us to carry. Sometimes we feel that we are wise to ruminate about how we have been wronged. Being bitter for decades is not accepting the suffering of Christ. When we are bitter, we are focused on our suffering, not Jesus' suffering. The good news is that God does not want us to carry the burden of the pain and consequences of others' actions any longer. He wants us to bring the debts that are owed to us and place them at the foot of the cross. We give that burden to Him and trust that He will take care of it in a just way.

FORGIVING OURSELVES

When we think about those we need to forgive, we often overlook forgiving ourselves for any egregious things we may have done. The term "forgive myself" helps folks realize they have not allowed themselves to be forgiven for their actions. Often people believe they need to suffer more for their wrongdoing. The trouble with this lie of the enemy is that a person can never fully suffer enough to feel forgiven or to be at peace with themselves and their world. If we could suffer enough to satisfy justice, we would not need a Savior to die for us. However, many are drawn into a self-inflicted suffering which creates a black hole in the heart that can never be satisfied.

Cynthia's husband told me that he felt it was Cynthia's abortion that was causing the problems they were having. One evening, after we had shown a video at our home for a small group of friends, Cynthia stayed and visited with my wife and me. In the middle of the conversation, the Holy Spirit told me to wade into the abortion issue with Cynthia. I asked her, "Do you think that the abortion you had has affected you?"

Cynthia replied, "No, that was before I was a Christian. When I came to Christ, He forgave me of all my sins."

The Spirit gave me the next question that uncovered the real problem: Have you forgiven yourself? Immediately Cynthia began to sob, and I knew that the Spirit had touched the spot in her life that was causing her so much pain. At this point I explained that if there is one sin that Jesus' blood cannot cleanse, then His blood is insufficient to cover any sin. To insist that we have to suffer for our sin is a denial of the gospel of Christ. That was all it took. Cynthia forgave herself. God set her heart free, and she remains free to this day.

"Forgiving myself" is not saying to myself that what I did was okay or that I can let this go. In our hearts, we demand justice, even for our own egregious acts. Because of this natural instinct for justice, the enemy finds it easy to persuade us to deny God's forgiveness and, instead, choose to suffer a little first.

If I took another man's life, how would I forgive myself? I can't actually pay the debt I owe to my victim. Doing time in jail is not enough to satisfy the demand for justice in my heart or in his family's hearts. It would take an infinite sacrifice that only the God-man Jesus Christ provides. Mere human suffering is insufficient.

Therefore, to forgive myself, I must place the debt I owe at the foot of the cross and trust that Jesus' blood will satisfy the demands of justice the enemy and my internal instincts level at me. If I believe the enemy's lie that I can somehow suffer enough to satisfy that demand for justice, then I will spend the rest of my life trying to pay that debt. If I renounce that lie and embrace the truth that my sin has been fully and completely satisfied by Jesus, then I can be at peace and set free. While society may demand more from me in satisfaction of justice for my actions, I can be at peace with God even while paying my debt to society.

FORGIVING GOD

The concept of forgiving God may be difficult to wrap our minds around. It seems ludicrous to forgive God when He is the One who is perfect and holy. Nonetheless, there are times in life when God does not meet a need we fully expect, and the end result is feeling let down by Him. The real problem stems from believing lies about God's character. This lack of understanding who He is, coupled with believing lies of the enemy, affects our perception of His actions toward us and causes doubts in our thinking.

If we are victims of spiritual abuse—the oppression of law without love, or guilt without grace and forgiveness—we can perceive God to be at the heart of that abuse and blame Him for it. Then God becomes part of the problem and we feel there is no place left to go for relief. When this happens, we can get stuck in that resentment and bitterness for decades. But we don't have to stay there. To get free, we simply repent, renounce the lies of the enemy regarding how we perceived God has let us down, and ask Him to set our hearts free of the lies that led to the bitterness and resentment.

For God so loved the world that he gave his one and only Son, that whoever believes in him shall not perish but have eternal life (John 3:16).

When we "forgive God" for not acting like we expected Him to, we in effect are renouncing the lies of the enemy that led to that resentment and are embracing the truth of God in all His holiness.

You may need some time to ponder this important step. Let me encourage you to peel back the lies and pursue the truth. You will be amazed just how freeing it is to actually change your mind about God (forgive God) and the pain you perceive He caused you (See Job 1:22; 2:10). Ask God if there is any resentment you are hiding in your heart toward Him. He is faithful and will reveal it to you when you ask with an open and sincere heart.

BREAKING THE CONTRACTS

You can use the freedom protocol to ask God to void any bitterness contracts with the enemy. We are not talking about a recipe as if we are making cookies. There are no magic words. I have used carefully crafted words to give understanding to the concepts here, but with God, He is more concerned about our hearts than our words. It is about coming to God, asking Him to lawfully void the contracts we have renounced. It is about asking Him to set us free from the lies and binding contracts that have kept us in a state of bitterness and bondage.

In whatever way we do this, with whatever words we use to convey these thoughts, we will find freedom. Freedom follows when we surrender these painful events to God and forgive the offender from the heart. If we are still harassed and tormented by the enemy after doing this, then we go to God again, and ask Him to reveal any additional lies and contracts that need to be addressed. God promises to meet us where we are and lead us to freedom. However, He can't unjustly intervene to lawfully set us free from a contract with which we are still in agreement. Don't expect God to trespass on the property you and the enemy share. It is the truth that will set you free. Be ruthless with yourself in exposing the lies and in believing the truth, and you will be amazed at how God will use that truth to set your heart free.

The freedom protocol works for any issue on which you find yourself being harassed and tormented by the enemy, such as immorality, pride, hypocrisy, addictions, anger, profanity, rebellion, low self-esteem, impatience, and greed.

This approach works because every besetting sin (binding contract with the enemy) in our life is based on a lie. The remedy for every sin has been provided by God in age-old principles of law,[67] which demand that any contract formed on the basis of a lie is void *ab initio* (to the beginning) at the point where we renounce the lie and believe and embrace the truth. This allows God to justly and lawfully void our binding contracts and to set us free without unjustly trespassing on the enemy's property, or rights (his contracts with us). God can lawfully stand at the door of our hearts and justly protect us and the contracts we have with Him. Living under God's protection and being bound in contract with Him is living the abundant life Jesus describes in the scriptures:

> *The thief comes only to steal and kill and destroy; I came that they may have life, and have it abundantly (John 10:10 NASB).*

---

67. "The Avalon Project: Documents in Law, History and Diplomacy." Yale Law School Lillian Goldman Law Library. 2008. https://avalon.law.yale.edu/ancient/hamframe.asp. See "The Avalon Project" for other forms of ancient law.

PART 2:

Practical Applications

Chapter Eleven:

Let's Get Started

By now you are probably wondering, "Now what? Where do I start and how can I apply what I've learned?" This chapter is devoted to helping you practically apply the freedom protocol to issues or sin you are struggling with. Even now, there may be something you know God is tugging at your heart to acknowledge. When you see that the freedom protocol is in agreement with God's way of setting you free from the power of sin, peace will be resident in your heart.

BEFORE WE BEGIN, PREPARE YOUR HEART

ASK GOD FOR HELP

Before you begin, pray for God's help in this process. You can use the following prayer as a guide to help you get started:

"Lord, I acknowledge that I have sinned and given the enemy authority in my life by believing his lies. I repent from that way of life. As I begin this process, give me discernment regarding the truth about my sin and the enemy's lies. I renounce his lies and ask You to break the enemy's strongholds and contracts in my life. I also ask You to take back the access and authority I gave to the enemy by believing him. I choose to return that access and authority to You. Please watch over my heart and continue to teach me the truth that will set me free. In Jesus' Name, Amen."

ASSESSMENT

It's important to take some time to assess your heart to discover your expectations. Many see their issues in life as a huge mountain looming before them. *Where do we start?* When it comes to your spiritual walk with God, the focus should primarily be on the *journey* and not just the *destination*. I can travel from Los Angeles, California, to Denver, Colorado, and make the trip in about sixteen hours. If I focus on the destination only, I will miss places like Death Valley, the Grand Canyon, and beautiful mountain spots in Utah and Colorado, all because I was focused on getting to my destination, Denver. But if I took five days instead of pushing sixteen hours to make the trip, how much more rewarding and satisfying would it be?

There is much to gain on this path and much to learn about God and about yourself. Take time to appreciate the journey you are on with Him. Witness God and His majesty as He works in your life. Slowing down will be the most wonderful part of the journey. If you try to race through it, you'll miss getting to know the One who is your remedy. We all want love, peace, joy and all the other fruits of the Spirit.[68] It will take patience to discover a new way to live. We simply need a starting point to begin this journey with God.

IDENTIFY AN AREA OF HARASSMENT

Some contracts we have with the enemy are more obvious than others. Let's start with the areas of your life that seem out of control or subject to harassment, areas where you find little relief from constant temptation. I'm talking about those little things you may have been thinking about while reading the previous chapters. If you are having difficulty deciding, ask God for help on what to focus on first.

---

68. See I Corinthians 12.

As you choose an area of focus, do not let the enemy discourage you with more of his lies. He does not want you to be free. He will lie to you in these or similar ways:

- This is just too much to handle or too difficult.

- You are too deep into this sin to think there is any hope you can change.

- Pick ten things to work on and get your life fixed all at once.

- This is going to take more effort than you are able to give, and it probably isn't going to work anyway.

Remember that the enemy's goal is to keep you from trying. Stay on course and remain committed to the process.

Pick a constant source of harassment that discourages you. If you are dealing with addictions, recognize there are generally two components to every addiction:

1. The physical part which may take several weeks to get the substance completely out of your system, and

2. The emotional part which can outlast the physical presence of the substance in your system and will at times create fear.

As a counselor, I would not advise starting with a substance addiction because it is often better to experience some success before tackling life-controlling issues. Some may be ready to dive right into the addiction, and some may not be ready. The enemy's goal is to get you to give up, causing you to abandon the whole process. Ask God, "What do You want me to start working on first?" Then listen and wait for His answer.

Once you have identified the area of focus, it's time to dive in—let's get started.

FREEDOM PROTOCOL

1.   Identify the lie(s) of the enemy you believed.[69]

2.   Identify the respective truth(s) as revealed by God.

3.   Repent (change your mind) from believing the lies to believing the truth.

4.   Renounce the lies and embrace the truth as revealed by God.

5.   Take back the access you granted to the enemy by believing his lies.

6.   Return that access back to God and ask Him to protect you from the enemy.

1. IDENTIFY THE LIE(S)

"Therefore, laying aside falsehood, speak truth each one of you with his neighbor, for we are members of one another" (Eph. 4:25 NASB).

"Ask, and it shall be given you; seek, and ye shall find; knock, and it shall be opened unto you" (Matt. 7:7 KJV).

What are the lies you have believed over the years regarding the identified issue, or area of focus? This is not a work to do alone. Listen for God's voice as you search for the lies. He has a vested interest in your success. He will help you discover them, so listen to what He is telling you throughout the process. It's imperative to write down what the Lord reveals, and to be prepared to jot down unrelated ideas He gives you. (It's helpful to keep the unrelated ideas on a separate piece of paper.)

Remember the two kinds of lies with which you will be dealing:

*   Circumstantial Lies: these are lies specific to the moment or circumstance at the time of your struggle:
    *   This is too difficult.
    *   One more time won't hurt.
    *   You can start tomorrow.

---

69. One can start with identifying the lie(s) or the truth(s)—but before moving on to step three, it is best to identify both the lie(s) and the truth(s).

- Foundational Lies: these are lies believed for many years:
  - You can't trust anyone.
  - No one else has the kinds of problems you have.
  - You are not as good as other people.

Recognizing the circumstantial lies is a bit easier than identifying the foundational lies because it's difficult to recognize a lie you've believed for so many years. The Holy Spirit will bring into question that which you have previously believed as true. Let Him challenge your thinking about the lie(s) and the truth(s).

Nearly 2,000 years ago Jesus explained how the Holy Spirit would work in our hearts and minds:

> *"When the Advocate comes, whom I will send to you from the Father—the Spirit of truth who goes out from the Father—he will testify about me" (John 15:26; emphasis mine).*

> *"But when he, the Spirit of truth, comes, he will guide you into all the truth. He will not speak on his own; he will speak only what he hears, and he will tell you what is yet to come" (John 16:13; emphasis mine).*

As you begin to identify the lies, it will be helpful if you imagine the enemy saying *It's okay to do this because . . .* The enemy's lies are almost always a justification for why you can yield to his temptations. Keep this in mind as you work through every issue. Don't be afraid to go deep and ask God to reveal additional lies that are related to that specific temptation or issue in your life.

Let's get to work. Grab a piece of paper or download the "Breaking Enemy Strongholds" PDF worksheet.[70] It's a good idea to use one sheet of paper for each stronghold/contract. This will keep things organized and also leave room to add additional lies and truth to the specific stronghold/contract. Take your time. Do not be

---

70. *Healing for the Heart Ministries.* "Breaking Enemy Strongholds." https://h4hm.org/book-resources

anxious. Just let the Holy Spirit speak to your mind and heart. This cannot be forced. Focus on the journey not just the destination.

Writing down what God reveals gives you a way to keep track of the insights as you address each lie[71] of the enemy. Please keep these three things in mind as you begin: 1) don't worry about the truth yet, just focus on identifying the lies, 2) don't be overwhelmed with the number of lies God reveals to you, and 3) don't get hung up trying to decide if something is a lie or the truth. This is a process and it will take some time to complete. The thing to do now is get the thoughts moving from your mind to paper; you will sort out the lies and truths later in the process.

Breathe a short prayer asking God to help you as you move forward. For example:

Dear Lord,

Please help me as I search for lies in my life and help me discern the truth that will set me free. I trust You to give me just what I can handle. Send Your Holy Spirit to speak truth into my heart and life. Amen.

2. IDENTIFY THE TRUTH(S)

And all things, whatsoever ye shall ask in prayer, believing, ye shall receive (Matt. 21:22 NASB).

Do not lie to one another, since you laid aside the old self with its evil practices, and have put on the new self who is being renewed to a true knowledge according to the image of the One who created him" (Col. 3:9-10 NASB).

Generally, the truth is more than just the opposite of the lie. Let the Holy Spirit speak freely to you about the truth. Make sure the

---

71. If you get stuck thinking about lies, try using other words like statements, tales, or story lines of the enemy.

truth you are embracing is consistent with God's word. The enemy is an expert in getting you to rationalize by justifying a lie as the truth. Remember that it is the truth that sets you free, so this is a very critical part of the freedom protocol.

3-4. REPENT AND RENOUNCE

Repent, then, and turn to God, so that he will forgive your sins (Acts 3:19 Good News Translation, GNT).

The apostles left and started telling everyone to turn to God (Mark 6:12 Contemporary English Version, CEV).

Therefore, having put away falsehood, let each one of you speak the truth with his neighbor, for we are members one of another (Eph. 4:25 ESV).

Another critical part of the freedom protocol is repentance (changing your mind). You can acknowledge the truth and feel guilty for having believed the lie, but nothing will take place until you actually change your mind from believing the lie to believing the truth. Simply knowing that you ought to change your mind does not work. Even wanting to change your mind does not work. It takes action on your part to change your mind. One way to do this is to renounce the lie as a lie of the enemy and believe and embrace the truth. If the lie involves pleasure, then the choice can be more difficult. This kind of lie says that pleasure is more important than the truth in the moment. Here, you are at a crisis of belief. You will either choose pleasure over the truth and remain in bondage to the enemy, or you will choose truth over pleasure and allow God to void those contracts and set you free. Before you begin working through these lies, let's talk about what it looks like to embrace the truth.

*These are the things that you shall do: Speak the truth to one an-
other; render in your gates judgments that are true and make for
peace (Zech. 8:16 ESV).*

*Do your best to present yourself to God as one approved, a worker
who has no need to be ashamed, rightly handling the word of truth
(II Tim. 2:15).*

Sanctify them by the truth; your word is truth (John 17:17).

God is inviting you to change your thinking. The clearer your
thinking is between the lies and the truth, the easier it is to believe
and embrace the truth.

Be deliberate as you identify the truth. There is no need to skimp
on the truth when associating the truth with each lie.

Now that you have the lie(s) and truth(s) identified and docu-
mented, you are ready to be lawfully set free from the lie-filled contracts of the enemy.

5-6. TAKE BACK AND GIVE

*Therefore be imitators of God, as beloved children; and walk in love,
just as Christ also loved you and gave Himself up for us, an offering
and a sacrifice to God as a fragrant aroma (Eph. 5:1-2 NASB).*

*Give me your heart, my son, And let your eyes delight in my ways
(Prov. 23:26).*

*Let the peace of Christ rule in your hearts, to which indeed you were
called in one body; and be thankful (Col. 3:15 ESV).*

Because you have believed the lies of the enemy and have entered
into contracts with him, you have granted the enemy certain access
rights. You now have lawful authority to take back the ground, or
access rights, you were deceived into giving him when you believed

his lies. You can now give those access rights back to God and ask Him to watch over your heart.

When you are ready, go to God in prayer. Find a quiet place where you will not be disturbed and get rid of any distractions. Take some time to prepare your heart and ask God to be with you as you move forward. With the list of lies and truths you've identified, start praying through each one. In an unrushed manner, ask God to void the contracts you made with the enemy and ask Him to protect His property rights (your heart and the contract you now have with Him). Here is a sample prayer:

"Lord I acknowledge and repent of (The Sin) and for believing the enemy's lie that ___ (The Lie) ___, by which I granted him access to, and authority in, my life. I renounce the lie. I ask you to void the lie-filled contract to which I agreed by believing his lies. I choose to believe the truth that (The Truth) . I take back the access and authority to my heart I gave the enemy by believing his lie, and I return that access and authority to You."

When you are finished with the entire list, talk to God about what you have just done. You may find the following ideas helpful as you surrender your heart to the truth:

1. Tell the Lord you are done with this sin and the enemy's lies.

2. Ask the Lord if there are any more lies about this sin He wants to reveal to you. If there are no more lies, go to point 4 below.

3. If more lies are revealed to you, jot them down. Discover what the truth is. Pray through that newly revealed lie and truth. When you are done with that new lie, return to point 2 above.

4. Ask God to show you in some way that you are free of all the contracts regarding that particular sin. In your mind's eye He may give you confirmation through a song, a picture, a scripture, or a quotation. This will be meaningful to you personally because your Creator knows you.

5. If nothing happens when you work through point 4 above, be patient. Often you can be prompted at a later time when it is unexpected. God is incredibly creative, and He will do something that will bless you more than you could ever imagine.

Be sure to jot down what God shows you during your prayer time so you can recall the moment He told you that you were clean and free. When the enemy tries to remind you of the past, remind him that these strongholds/contracts are now void and then ask God to intervene to protect you. It might also be helpful to remind the enemy of his future.

Some have been discouraged when a few months later God brings up new issues or highlights additional lies related to the contracts that have been renounced and voided. God is gracious not to bring up everything at once. If He did, we would surely be overwhelmed by the process. Remember, this is a journey. Trust God's perfect timing in dealing with all of the contracts in your life. If another lie is revealed to you, take courage and pray through it.

When you have renounced the lies, believed and embraced the truth, and asked God to void the contracts related to the specific sin with which you struggle, you'll notice an absence of harassment by the enemy. If, in the future, you believe another lie just add that lie to the list, pray through it, replace it with the truth, and then move forward in freedom. The more you discern and work through these lies, the easier it will be to renounce them and experience the peace that immediately comes by embracing the truth.

WHO IS RESPONSIBLE FOR YOUR SUCCESS?

God has a vested interest in your success because He wants you to rule over sin, to be free from the enemy, and to be with Him for eternity. When you rely on His authority, He will see you through.

There are at least two things God wishes to accomplish in your life. It's important to understand them both:

1. *God wants to clean up your past, all your sin and failures.* He does this by exchanging your polluted history with the perfect history of Jesus Christ. When you embrace Jesus and His sacrifice for your past and future, God declares you not guilty. In a moment you stand before God just as if you never sinned (see chapter 6, Remedy #1). All this was accomplished for you 2,000 years ago. It was done for you before you were born. It is finished and complete, and God is holding this cleansing out to you for you to embrace. It is there for the taking.

2. *God wants to restore you into His image by replacing the lies you have believed with the truth.* But if God were to expose you to every lie you have ever believed at one moment, it would destroy you. He is not interested in destroying you. He wants to deliver you from the power of sin (Remedy #2), give you the abundant life, and help you grow to love the truth. This is the work of a lifetime as He unravels the lies you have believed, one by one, in the order He chooses and in His own timing.

People have often exclaimed they have millions of lies they have believed over the years and they just don't know where to start. This may be true, but the lie of the enemy wrapped in this truth is that *you might just as well not deal with any of it because there is too much to handle.* Yes, it can be overwhelming to sort through the millions of lies you have believed. Fortunately for us, our salvation is not based on cleaning up all the lies we have believed over the years. If it were, we certainly would be overwhelmed and crushed by the weight of the task. Our salvation is based on the finished work of Jesus on the cross on our behalf.

Deal with each lie God reveals to you *as He reveals it*. Don't overwhelm yourself with all the lies of the past, just focus on the lie(s) He shows you today (NOW). Remember, He has already cleansed your past. You are not doing this work so that God will save you. You are doing this work because He has saved you, because you want to begin thinking like God thinks, and because you want continual deliverance from the enemy's lies that are affecting your life.

If you do find yourself feeling overwhelmed, keep your focus on the healer, not the disease. Martin Luther said:

> *"When I look at myself, I don't see how I could possibly be saved. When I look at Christ, I don't see how I could possibly be lost."*

Trust that God has your best interest at heart. Let Him set the pace, and you will find yourself agreeing with the apostle Paul:

> *"And I am certain that God, who began the good work within you, will continue his work until it is finally finished on the day when Christ Jesus returns" (Phil. 1:6 NLT).*

God knows just how much to bring to your attention so you can exercise His remedies and get free (rule over sin), while at the same time ensuring you're not overwhelmed by the immensity of the task. It is God's job to clean up the messes and bring about the change that glorifies Him. Our job is to deal with what He gives us today.

WHO VOIDS THE CONTRACTS?

As you begin to rule over sin in your life, you will likely hear several new lies of the enemy:

- You can sin all you want and then just break the contract afterwards.[72]

- This feels pretty powerful.

- You are doing pretty well now.

- You really have power and authority over the enemy.

- If you work really hard on this, you can be perfect.

God is the only one who can lawfully void the contracts you have with the enemy, but be careful, the enemy is sly. Don't be tricked into believing you can force the enemy to obey you. It is God who enforces the voided contract and forces the enemy to get permission before he can gain access to your life. Never forget from where your victory comes.

"I have told you these things, so that in me you may have peace. In this world you will have trouble. But take heart! I have overcome the world" (John 16:33).

But thanks be to God! He gives us the victory through our Lord Jesus Christ (I Cor. 15:57).

For no word from God will ever fail (Luke 1:37).

Therefore, since we are surrounded by such a great cloud of witnesses, let us throw off everything that hinders and the sin that so

---

72. The scripture never makes provision for willful, deliberate, or unrepentant sin. This way of dealing with sin stems from the dark ages where sin was seen mostly as a transaction that needed correction. The truth is that sin is relational, and it wounds the object of our love. While God has provided the remedy for sin and the power of sin, He does not tolerate a willful life of sin. Our attitudes toward sin will need a lie/truth adjustment during our journey with God.

easily entangles. And let us run with perseverance the race marked out for us (Heb. 12:1).

No, in all these things we are more than conquerors through him who loved us (Rom. 8:37).

But you, Lord, are a shield around me, my glory, the One who lifts my head high (Ps. 3:3).

The light shines in the darkness, and the darkness has not overcome it (John 1:5).

Who is it that overcomes the world? Only the one who believes that Jesus is the Son of God (I John 5:5).

You, dear children, are from God and have overcome them, because the one who is in you is greater than the one who is in the world (I John 4:4).

The LORD is my light and my salvation— whom shall I fear? The LORD is the stronghold of my life— of whom shall I be afraid? (Ps. 27:1).

"For I am the LORD your God who takes hold of your right hand and says to you, do not fear; I will help you" (Isa. 41:13).

Cast all your anxiety on him because he cares for you (I Peter 5:7).

I can do all this through him who gives me strength (Phil. 4:13).

Trust in the LORD with all your heart and lean not on your own understanding; in all your ways submit to him, and he will make your paths straight (Prov. 3:5-6).

And he said, "These are they who have come out of the great tribulation; they have washed their robes and made them white in the blood of the Lamb" (Rev. 7:14).

Chapter Twelve:

Pride and Humility

If you've come to this chapter having worked and prayed through the freedom protocol, you are already experiencing some freedom. The enemy is aware of his defeat and will be subtle in his attempts to bring you into bondage again. The following discussion of pride and humility is meant to be a word of caution, which will help in the midst of chaos, confusion, and conflict.

> *Humble yourselves, therefore, under God's mighty hand, that he may lift you up in due time (I Pet. 5:6).*
>
> *Humble yourselves before the Lord, and He will exalt you (James 4:10 ESV).*

Pride is a character trait easily identified in others because we have a natural aversion to pride we see in others. But humility is a bit more elusive. We appreciate it when we observe it in others and like to think of ourselves as being humble rather than prideful.

So how do you eliminate pride and become humble? Better yet, how do you humble yourself as James and Peter recommend in the above texts? It sounds like this is an intentional choice.

We cannot directly resolve issues of pride or achieve true humility by pursuing them directly. They are by-products. To show this, let's look for a moment at happiness.

Have you ever met anyone who went looking for happiness and actually found it? The world is filled with people who have tried to find it but are unsuccessful because happiness is an experience that can't *be found*. It's a by-product and comes as a result of hard work, a job well done, being appreciated, serving others, or finishing a big project. After pursuing meaningful activities, we are often surprised to discover that we are happy. Happiness is like a shadow, showing itself in ways that seem impossible to grasp. We spend years and much of our money chasing happiness only to have it elude our grasp time after time. The same concept is true of humility.

At the root of both pride and humility are two words with which we have become very familiar—lies and truth. Often, thoughts of humility direct us to a false humility, self-deprecating statements like I am a worm, I'm tainted by my past, I can't do anything right, and I'm not as good as others. Each one of these self-deprecating statements is rooted in a lie, which is one reason it is false humility.

So how do we become humble in the true sense of the word? The answer may be simple to understand but a bit more complex to implement. Let's look at what's going on internally and externally when pride and humility are present:

- Every time I believe a lie of the enemy, pride is at the center.

- Every time pride shows itself in my life, a lie of the enemy is at the center of that pride.

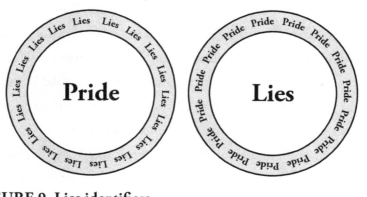

FIGURE 9. Lies identifiers

- Every time I believe and embrace the truth of God, humility is at the center.
- Every time humility shows itself in my life, the truth of God is at the center of that humility.

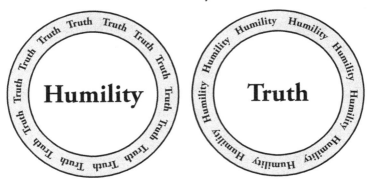

FIGURE 10. Truth identifiers

I challenge anyone to identify a lie of the enemy that, if believed, will make one humble. Likewise, try to produce one truth of God that, if believed, will make one prideful.

Let us say that algebra is really easy and intuitive for me. Is it the truth (I am naturally good at algebra) that makes me prideful? Or is it *a lie about that truth* that gets me into trouble? The truth itself does not cause me to be prideful. The lies of the enemy about the truth are what cause me to be prideful. Let's look at some examples:

The lie is: You are smarter or more special than others.
The truth is: Others have been gifted by God in different ways.

The lie is: This skill makes you better than other people.
The truth is: You are not defined by your skills but rather by your character.

The lie is: People who can't understand algebra are idiots.
The truth is: People are gifted differently.
The lie is: You did this all yourself.

The truth is: God is the source of all my abilities.

The lie is: My skills are given to me for my benefit.

The truth is: God gave me skills and talents to help me help others.

Humility comes when we believe and embrace the truth. It may be true that we excel at algebra. It may also be true that we had talented teachers who taught us algebra. If we accept the truth that all our talent and skill was given to us by our Creator to benefit others, we will be humble about our talents and skills. We may recognize that others do not perform as well at algebra, but if we also realize they excel in areas of their own, humility is at the heart of that thought.

This leads us to the first set of rules regarding pride and humility:

- Whenever we believe and embrace the lies of the enemy, pride is there.

- Whenever we believe and embrace the truth of God, humility is there.

When you are convicted of being prideful, search for and renounce the related lie.

Those who live in truth will be humble about both their identity and their accomplishments.

This leads us to the second set of rules regarding pride and humility:

- Pride always brings with it chaos, confusion, conflict, and temporary pleasure. These states of mind, heart, and circumstance are footprints of the enemy (see pages 102 and 103), and they evidence the presence of pride. When pride is present, there are lies at the center.

- Humility always brings with it peace, understanding, a teachable spirit, lasting joy, and harmony. These states of mind, heart, and circumstance are footprints of Jesus, and they evidence the presence of humility. When humility is present, there is truth at the center.

When pride comes, then comes disgrace, but with humility comes wisdom (Prov. 11:2).

Pride goes before destruction, a haughty spirit before a fall (Prov. 16:18).

Pride brings a person low, but the lowly in spirit gain honor (Prov. 29:23).

HOW DO PRIDE AND HUMILITY RELATE TO THE FREEDOM PROTOCOL AND GOD'S REMEDIES?

As you aggressively implement the freedom protocol and remedies we have described throughout these chapters, you will be dealing with lies and truth on a regular basis. It is important to understand that the stakes are high. The trail of pride leads to the enemy's footprints. Each lie we believe and its resulting pride will dramatically and negatively affect our relationships. The trail of humility leads to Jesus' footprints of peace and joy. The truth of God we believe and its resulting humility will dramatically and positively impact our relationships.[73]

We must also be aware that both lies and truth can be delivered to us in unexpected ways—sometimes from an enemy, a spouse, a child, a coworker, a song, or even a friend. I have found it helpful to consider pride and humility when I am trying to determine the source and how to respond.

By pursuing truth and renouncing lies, we find that life becomes more peaceful and full of joy. We all have our rough spots, but sooner or later the truth will have a dramatic impact on our lives and the lives of those we love.

---

73. It is true that in relationships there are those who will not give up conflict. In the midst of that conflict, one can have peace in their own heart regardless of the other's actions.

DEFENDING YOURSELF

It is a natural and reflexive action to defend ourselves and the lies we have believed when we are approached with a convicting truth. Some find it next to impossible to accept a new truth presented and are ready to fight to the death to defend or protect the lie. When this happens they will not find the relief they so badly desire. Some who are determined to win at all costs will trash their marriages and everyone around them to protect their pride and related lies. It is pride that prevents us from seeing other possibilities. To grow we must at least consider the possibility that we could be wrong. If we cannot, we will remain stuck. Our pride will drive us deeper into the lies and will ultimately lead us into isolation and drive away the ones we love.

The more we defend ourselves, the more the other party wants to convince us that we are wrong or that we did the wrong thing. When we are defending ourselves, we will hear *You think you are perfect, Everyone else is wrong but you, Why are you so hardheaded?* As we embrace the truth and own up to our errors and incorrect actions, others will try to soften the crash landing. We may hear them say *It wasn't that bad, Everybody makes mistakes, You'll do better next time.* And yet having experienced this mercy and hope from others, we still, more often than not, tend to defend ourselves and make room for pride and lies to take a foothold in our lives. If we want different results, it may be time to try a different strategy that can and will lead to humility instead of pride.

GOOD PRIDE

Is there such a thing as good pride like pride in our children's accomplishments or having done a good job? The problem is that language breaks down at times and does not convey our thoughts accurately. For example, I love God, my family, and chocolate. Is there a difference between loving God and loving chocolate? Certainly. When we are talking to friends, we understand the meaning of the word love without having to give an in-depth explanation each time we use it. The same thing applies to pride. When talking about our children's accomplishments, for example, we use the word pride. We can approach these accomplishments by believing lies of the enemy such as *I am the reason my children are so talented,* or *I did a good job because I'm smarter and more skilled than everyone else.* But these comments do not acknowledge the true source of these accomplishments. Generally, when we speak the truth and acknowledge God as the source of talent and skill, humility is the result. When we believe the lie that our talent and skill is all about us—pride is the result. I can take pride in my children's accomplishments and in my work as long as I believe and embrace the truth that God is the source of those accomplishments and skills in my life. Let's not get caught up in the word pride but rather, let's focus on embracing the truth, in every circumstance.

Chapter Thirteen:

Hardship and Trials

As you implement the freedom protocol, you could be lulled into thinking that by exercising these principles you will be free from hardship and trials. The truth is—you will still have both. Some trials come as a result of our own doing, when we've yielded to temptation, and some are allowed by God. When God tests us through trials, His motivation is for our refinement, growth, and success. This chapter is included to help you develop a healthy view of hardships and trials, and to help arm you with the knowledge that God has not abandoned you, and He can be trusted.

> *Blessed is the man who remains steadfast under trial, for when he has stood the test he will receive the crown of life, which God has promised to those who love him (James 1:12 ESV).*

> *Count it all joy, my brothers, when you meet trials of various kinds (James 1:2 ESV).*

> *Indeed, all who desire to live a godly life in Christ Jesus will be persecuted (II Tim. 3:12 ESV).*

> *Do not be anxious about anything, but in everything by prayer and supplication with thanksgiving let your requests be made known to God. And the peace of God, which surpasses all understanding, will guard your hearts and your minds in Christ Jesus (Phil. 4:6-7 ESV).*

THE HEART OF GOD

God's intentions toward us, His creation, are good and for our success. Everything He does is redemptive, always.

> *The LORD is for me; I will not fear; what can man do to me? (Ps. 118:6 NASB).*

> *"For I know the thoughts that I think toward you, says the Lord, thoughts of peace and not of evil, to give you a future and a hope" (Jer. 29:11 NKJV).*

> *"I have said these things to you, that in me you may have peace. In the world you will have tribulation. But take heart; I have overcome the world" (John 16:33 ESV).*

God has revealed His thoughts through scripture, and His thoughts are true, even in adversity. At the heart of every trial is a loving God, who is supporting our growth, building us up, and completing our maturity in Him. We may not feel this truth or even believe it during the hardship, but in the testing through trials, God is working out every difficulty for our redemption.

If you had an oak tree in your backyard and your ten-year-old daughter asked you to make a rope swing for her on that tree, what would be the first thing you would do after you finished the swing? You would test the swing's strength and ability to hold weight. You might even put the rope through a stress test, not to break it but to make sure it is strong enough to carry your daughter. Any hardships or trials we experience must be viewed in the context of Jeremiah 29:11. God does not allow anything into our lives to break us but to strengthen and redeem us, so we can receive and handle even more of His blessings.

God only desires to bless us, and He only uses hardships and trials as preparation for greater blessings He has in store. However, blessings that come without the necessary hardship, discipline, and character development one needs to handle those blessings often lead the one so blessed to destruction. But much like a person who obtains sudden wealth beyond the ability to manage it, we too are vulnerable to too much blessing all at once.

Israel's record in the book of Judges clarifies what happens when we have God's full blessing without hardship: we often forget about Him—the source of blessings—and wander away from Him. If we were to receive His full, unrestrained blessings without hardship, it could destroy us. If God allowed us to experience unrestrained hardship, this could destroy us as well. In hardships and trials, God protects us.

We have a loving God in heaven who has His hand on the throttle that regulates blessing and hardship in our lives. When the enemy is not interfering through unresolved contracts, God can, little by little, develop us to receive more and more of His blessing which results in our deliverance from sin, and not our destruction.

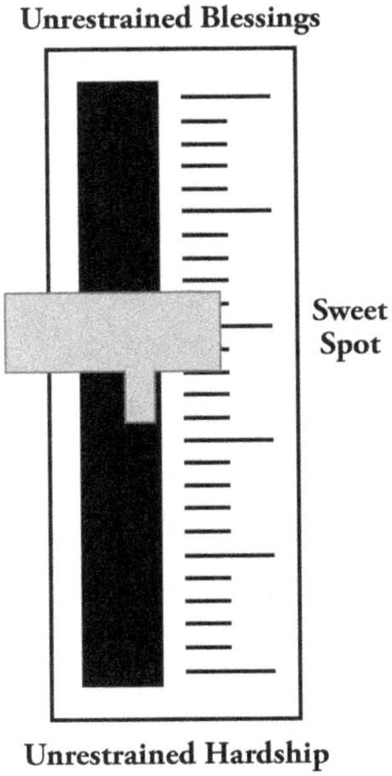

As we continue, let's review the following truths about God which will help us as we examine hardships and trials further:

- God is always just.

- God's motive is redemptive.

- God draws us toward Him; He never pushes us away.[74]

- God grows and matures us through hardships and trials.

- God's ultimate goal is to give us unrestrained blessing.

Unrestrained Blessings

Sweet Spot

Unrestrained Hardship

FIGURE 11.
Sweet Spot

---

74. Any separation between God and us happens when we pull away. Sometimes God will briefly pull away for the purpose of getting our attention, but His desire is always to draw us to Himself so that we may be redeemed.

Although we have the above truths, as sinners, we cannot be trusted with unrestrained blessing.

With every hardship and trial you will hear the enemy's lies:

- God is not acting justly toward me.

- God doesn't care about me or my situation.

- God is angry with me.

- God is trying to destroy me.

- God doesn't want to bless me.

- God wouldn't allow this trial to happen to me if He loved me.

HARDSHIP VERSUS TEMPTATION

Often hardship is confused with temptation. While one can just as equally give in to hardship as temptation, these are entirely different influences in our lives. Understanding the difference will be helpful moving forward.

Hardships are the difficult circumstances in life which happen to everyone. We experience hardship when we have financial setbacks, death and sickness, destroyed homes, dilapidated cars, unsuccessful businesses, etc. Jesus understood all these things are a part of life.

"I have said these things to you, that in me you may have peace. In the world you will have tribulation. But take heart; I have overcome the world" (John 16:33 ESV).

The first step in dealing with hardship is to realize that hardship happens to everyone, and we should not expect to be spared from it. The question is not about the nature of the hardship but about the nature of the One who has overcome the world and walks through that hardship with you.

Any contrary thoughts or beliefs to this truth are lies of the enemy. These lies are used to defame God's character and undermine our faith. At the core of every temptation that accompanies each hardship is a most important question: Can God be trusted? If you are unsettled in who God is then hardship and the associated temptation will be destructive and overwhelming. On the other hand, if you know God's character and are completely convinced that He loves and cares for you, you can go through that hardship with peace, even joy, in spite of the hardship.

You have doubtless witnessed someone who has gone through amazing hardship and declare they could've never endured without God. One person can experience hardship with amazing ease and grace, while others are completely destroyed by the same hardship. Some who are battling cancer praise God and rejoice in His love right up to the moment of their death; others become bitter and angry with Him, abandoning their faith and dying in their bitterness. What makes the difference is the response to the temptations about who God is.

You can choose to trust God and believe He is for you. You cannot force yourself to love God because love cannot be forced, but you can ask Him for the desire to love Him. Love is a relationship experience, and it is that experience with God's love that allows you to rely on Him and His wisdom when it comes to the hardships in life. Hardships are temporary but God is eternal.

If you find yourself white-knuckling your way through hardship, it's time to take a hard look at what you believe about God. Maybe it's time to renounce the enemy's lies you may have believed and embrace the truth about who God is.

THE ENEMY INTERFERES

Years ago I had a friend say something to me that had a powerful impact on my life. He said, "I see God blessing you and your family, but I also see the enemy snatching those same blessings away from you." For years I had missed God's goodness because I was focused on the work of the enemy. What if we apply all we've learned so far to the idea of God's blessings? Would we discover that our problem is not with God but with the contracts we have in place with the enemy, giving him the rights to snatch away those blessings?

Let's look at a contract Israel made with the enemy that robbed them of their blessings as recorded in Malachi 3:8-9, NASB:

> *"Will a man rob God? Yet you are robbing Me! But you say, 'How have we robbed You?' In tithes and offerings. You are cursed with a curse, for you are robbing Me, the whole nation of you!" (Mal. 3:8-9 NASB).*

Israel was robbing God of His tithes and offerings. However, God follows this rebuke with a promise and a challenge:

> *"Bring the whole tithe into the storehouse, so that there may be food in My house, and test Me now in this," says the LORD of hosts, "if I will not open for you the windows of heaven and pour out for you a blessing until it overflows" (Mal. 3:10 NASB).*

God challenged Israel to "test Me now in this." Israel had contracted with the enemy by taking the tithes which were to be given to God and spending them on themselves. Churches often quote these verses in Malachi when calling for the offering, but they seldom quote the following verse which is more powerful:

> *"Then I will rebuke the devourer for you, so that it will not destroy the fruits of the ground; nor will your vine in the field cast its grapes," says the LORD of hosts (Malachi 3:11 NASB).*

Like my friend suggested so many years ago, God was blessing me, but the devourer (the enemy) was destroying those blessings because of the agreements and contracts I had established with him.

God loved us so much that He gave us His only Son. So why doesn't God just rebuke the devourer all the time? This brings us back to the freedom protocol. Can a perfectly just God trespass on the enemy's contract rights and act unlawfully? Here lies the problem. Some of the hardships and trials we endure are the results of the agreements, or contracts, we have established with the enemy. God's justice does not permit Him to trespass on the contract rights we granted to the enemy in those binding contracts. When we renounce the enemy's lies and ask God to void those contracts, He will lawfully prevent the devourer from snatching blessings away from us.

As we move forward in our journey with God, we will always have the following two influences:

- Hardship and trials as *the result of our agreements, or contracts,* with the enemy. These contracts can be voided *ab initio* (back to the beginning).

- Hardship and trials as *strategically allowed into our lives by God.* God gently regulates that sweet spot between unrestrained blessing and unrestrained hardship—any circumstance He allows is for the purpose of helping us mature, so we can receive more of His blessings.

LIVING IN THE NOW

In time there is past, present, and future. There are some unique things about these three timeframes in our lives:

- God routinely dwells and exercises His power in the present (the NOW).

- The enemy routinely dwells and exercises his power in the past and the future.

Let's look at how God and the enemy relate to the past, present, and future.

HOW THE ENEMY WORKS

The Present: The enemy has little or no power, territory, or jurisdiction in the present. The enemy will always take a current situation and lie to us about it in the context of the past or the future. If you have a financial setback, for example, the enemy's focus is either on the past—God is justly or unjustly punishing you for your past deeds, or the future—you will be destroyed by your problem and lose everything. Rarely, in moments like this, do we thank God and confess that He is bigger than our hardships and setbacks, and that He already has a solution to the situation.

The Past: The enemy's focus on the past is generally about shame, guilt, and regret. He will tell us to give up, that there is no hope, that we've gone too far, and that our mistakes are too big to fix. He will offer half-truths, trying to convince us that God does not love us. As we seek to discover the lies of the enemy, we will soon discover they are full of accusations about our past. This is one half of the enemy's power, territory, and jurisdiction.

The Future: Many of the enemy's lies are about the future— what *might* happen or the worst-case scenario. In this case, the enemy focuses on things associated with fear, anxiety, and distrust of God. Generally, the things we fear are not real. As you think about this you will find that this applies to our relationships, activities, work, and spiritual life, among a host of other things. Then there is the desire to know what the future holds so there are no surprises, so we don't have to trust God. This is the other half of the enemy's power, territory, and jurisdiction.

Evaluate each lie that God discloses to you and discover for yourself how many lies minimize the present (NOW) and emphasize the past or future. If you are experiencing pain from the past, or fear or anxiety regarding the future, you can rule over the pain, fear, and anxiety by choosing to live in the NOW, trusting God with the past and future and exercising the freedom protocol with each lie of the enemy.

HOW GOD WORKS

The Present: God is all powerful and therefore owns the past, the present, and the future. The present is where God lives. He is the eternal present One. The Great I AM. All time is in the present tense to Him and He is always in the NOW with us. God loves to demonstrate His power in all time segments, but the NOW is where the journey with God begins and ends. Since lies involve using smoke and mirror tactics, Satan has little or no power in the NOW, which is reality or the truth. Reality and truth form the basis of God's territory and jurisdiction. If you are going through a hardship, God wants you to trust Him in the NOW for a solution. In moments like these, we can immediately thank God that He is bigger than our problem and that He already has a solution to our situation.

The Past: God does not want us to live with shame, guilt, and regret. In fact, He sent His only Son to rescue us from shame, guilt, regret, and death. He did this so He could give us life and cleanse us from the pollution of our past. All our sin has been paid for by His Son two thousand years ago. When God speaks to us of the past, it is for the purpose of cleaning it up and giving us new life. The Holy Spirit will never take away our hope, tell us we've gone too far, or that God doesn't love us. As we begin to listen to the voice of God in the midst of the enemy's lies, we will begin to tell the difference between the enemy's voice and God's comforting voice of peace and truth.

The Future: God wants us to trust Him and to believe with our hearts that He will always do what is best for us. Trust is something that comes as a result of relationship. It is part of the journey that God is taking with us. The first thing nearly every angel in scripture says to a man or woman they appear to is, "Fear not." God does not want us to be afraid. With whatever we might be faced, He is bigger than all of it. God wants us to trust Him with every aspect of our lives—our relationships, activities, work, and spiritual life, to mention a few. When He wants us to know certain things about the future, He will give us a prophetic revelation so we won't be taken by surprise and give up in despair. Remember that everything God does for His people is redemptive.

TABLE 6. Past, now, and future

	PAST	**NOW**	**FUTURE**
SATAN	Satan's power resides in our guilt, shame, and regret. He lies to us about God's forgiveness and cleansing.	Satan's power is nil in the NOW. Conflict is usually based on the past and future.	Satan's power resides in our anxiety and fear, causing us to distrust God.
GOD	God erases our past by forgiving us completely. We must believe and accept His forgiveness.	God lives and works in the NOW.	God invites us to trust Him with our future and be anxious for nothing.

HARDSHIP COMES JUST BEFORE FREEDOM

In the Bible, the first three chapters in Exodus tell of Israel's oppression of slavery in Egypt and God's plan to set them free. In chapter five Moses demands that Pharaoh let Israel go into the wilderness to hold a festival to God for three days. At this point in the story, Israel is focused on and excited about the freedom that is soon to be theirs. However, Pharaoh decides that Israel has too much time on their hands and orders them to do the same amount of work and, now, get their own straw to make the bricks. There is a freedom principle here we should remember: **just before we get free, things get tougher because the enemy does not want to let us go.**

If we forget this truth, we may prematurely give up in despair.

Thomas Edison had this perspective: "Many of life's failures are people who did not realize how close they were to success when they gave up."

There is a real battle over our souls, just as there was a real battle over the souls of the Israelites between Moses and Pharaoh. If you lose sight of the battle that is going on for your soul, you will be tempted to give up, sometimes just yards from the finish line.

We can never be free if we do not directly confront the enemy and the contracts that bind us. No matter how we might wish it to be different, being free requires a confrontation with the enemy of our souls just as Moses confronted Pharaoh. It is by this confrontation that God is able to demonstrate His power in our lives just as He did for Israel. This is how He lets us know from whom and what we have been set free. For us to get free from the enemy, we cannot be passive. In the Exodus story, God freed Israel. All they had to do was follow His lead and trust Him. If you think this is easy, read the rest of Exodus and see how Israel did.

PRODUCING FRUIT BRINGS ABOUT HARDSHIP

As we begin to rule over sin, God will begin to produce fruit in our lives. When the branches are connected to the vine, they cannot help but produce fruit. Producing fruit is not meant to be a white-knuckle experience; yet at times, this does bring about hardship. When God begins to produce fruit in our lives, people around us will respond in one of two ways:

- Some will embrace what has been happening in our lives, encourage us, and will likely begin a journey of their own with God.

- Others who have been white-knuckling their way through life with little or no fruit to show for their efforts will likely become jealous, discourage us, and begin to come against us.

I have heard it said, "The only trees at which people throw rocks are the ones with fruit."

As God begins to produce fruit in our lives, we should expect hardship and not be surprised if it comes from those we love. The enemy will be diligent to get us back into bondage with him. However, when we are free of the enemy's contracts on a particular issue, we live our lives with God standing at the door of our hearts, protecting us from the enemy's temptations on that issue. When God does allow the enemy to tempt us, it will always be with pa-rameters or limitations. We will not need to face the enemy alone.

We can read the Exodus story and see all the problems Israel had, and miss seeing the way God provided for them. We can also read the Exodus story and see all the amazing things God did for Israel and be surprised that Israel complained at every turn. It is easy for us to think we would behave differently, but as we already know, trust in God does not come naturally. Read the story and determine to trust God no matter where He leads. Remember, He will always do what is best for us. If we stay in the NOW, renouncing every lie of the enemy as they become known to us, and embrace the truth which God reveals, we will have amazing victory and fruit in our lives. Ruling over sin is not for the faint of heart. It is time for men and women of God to stand up and take their rightful and responsible place in the body of Christ and demonstrate to the world what the abundant life really looks like and how to truly live it—NOW.

MARTYRDOM

What about martyrs? If we follow the freedom protocol and exercise the remedies God has put in place, will we be protected from being martyrs? Our salvation is not just about our comfort and well-being. It is meant to be seed planted in the lives of others, a seed which will grow and ultimately bring others into a trusting relationship with God. This is true fruitfulness.

If you have not read John Foxe's book about martyrs,[75] I recommend it. This book talks about the many martyrs who gave their lives willingly, even joyfully, because they would not renounce their love and allegiance to their Lord Jesus Christ. It's astonishing how these individuals faced torture and agonizing death with peace and joy. Often those who were burned at the stake would sing and praise God while flames destroyed their bodies. Isn't it profound that these ordinary people had such amazing trust in God that they gave their lives so that others would come to know Jesus? Yet, not one drop of a martyr's blood was wasted by God. Every time a martyr was murdered or burned at the stake because of their fidelity to Jesus Christ, many more searching souls surrendered their lives to Him.

75. John Foxe, *The Acts and Monuments of the Church: Containing the History and the Sufferings of the Martyrs* (London: Scott, Webster, and Geary, 1838). View the PDF at *Healing for the Heart Ministries*: https://h4hm.org/book-resources.

As we think about being martyrs, fear and dread will doubtless set in. These feelings have no validity in the NOW but are focused on the future. We must remember that if God calls us to give our lives that others might live, He will give us the grace to face that trial at that moment. Hope, peace, and joy are ours as we remain in the NOW. If a martyr's faith is asked of us, a martyr's faith will be given us. Let's keep in mind that Jesus, who lived among us without sin, died a horrible death at the hands of those He came to save. But by His death, billions have come to know and accept Him. At the very end, when He felt the Father forsake Him for the first time because of our sins, in the final moments of His life, scripture records that

> *Jesus called out with a loud voice, "Father, into your hands I commit my spirit." When he had said this, he breathed his last"* (Luke 23:46).

At the very end, Jesus trusted the Father with His life and His future because He knew and understood the Father's character. Jesus invites us to enter into that same trust relationship with Him and the Father.

SCRIPTURES TO REVIEW DURING HARDSHIP

The lie of the enemy will always be that God is withholding good from you, His love is not big enough to overcome your trial and, in the end, He will abandon you; therefore, you must handle the hardship on your own. Yet, the truth is that we are called to endure trials at times for the purpose of God demonstrating His majesty and glory in our lives.

> *As he went along, he saw a blind man from birth. His disciples asked him, "Rabbi, who sinned, this man or his parents, that he was born blind?" "Neither this man nor his parents sinned," said*

Jesus, "but this happened so that the works of God might be displayed in him" (John 9:1-3).

His love for us is never ending and He will never leave or forsake us. When times of hardship and trial come, and they surely will, take heart and review the following scriptures regularly:

"I have said these things to you, that in me you may have peace. In the world you will have tribulation. But take heart; I have overcome the world" (John 16:33 ESV).

I will rejoice and be glad in Your lovingkindness, because You have seen my affliction; You have known the troubles of my soul, and You have not given me over into the hand of the enemy; You have set my feet in a large place (Ps. 31:7-8 NASB).

And after you have suffered a little while, the God of all grace, who has called you to his eternal glory in Christ, will himself restore, confirm, strengthen, and establish you (I Pet. 5:10 ESV).

Trust in the Lord with all your heart, and do not lean on your own understanding. In all your ways acknowledge him, and he will make straight your paths (Prov. 3:5-6 ESV).

Beloved, do not be surprised at the fiery trial when it comes upon you to test you, as though something strange were happening to you (I Pet. 4:12 ESV).

Even though I walk through the valley of the shadow of death, I will fear no evil, for you are with me; your rod and your staff, they comfort me (Ps. 23:4 ESV).

When the righteous cry for help, the Lord hears and delivers them out of all their troubles. The Lord is near to the brokenhearted and saves the crushed in spirit (Ps. 34:17-18 ESV).

Many are the afflictions of the righteous, but the Lord delivers him out of them all (Ps. 34:19 ESV).

Submit yourselves therefore to God. Resist the devil, and he will flee from you (James 4:7 ESV).

Through him we have also obtained access by faith into this grace in which we stand, and we rejoice in hope of the glory of God. Not only that, but we rejoice in our sufferings, knowing that suffering produces endurance, and endurance produces character, and character produces hope, and hope does not put us to shame, because God's love has been poured into our hearts through the Holy Spirit who has been given to us (Rom. 5:2-5 ESV).

Blessed be the God and Father of our Lord Jesus Christ, the Father of mercies and God of all comfort, who comforts us in all our affliction, so that we may be able to comfort those who are in any affliction, with the comfort with which we ourselves are comforted by God (II Cor. 1:3-4 ESV).

Then the Lord knows how to rescue the godly from trials, and to keep the unrighteous under punishment until the day of judgment (II Pet. 2:9 ESV).

For this light momentary affliction is preparing for us an eternal weight of glory beyond all comparison (II Cor. 4:17 ESV).

And they have no root in themselves, but endure for a while; then, when tribulation or persecution arises on account of the word, immediately they fall away (Mark 4:17 ESV).

Though the fig tree does not bud and there are no grapes on the vines, though the olive crop fails and the fields produce no food, though there are no sheep in the pen and no cattle in the stalls, yet I will rejoice in the Lord, I will be joyful in God my Savior. The Sovereign Lord is my strength (Hab. 3:17-19).

Chapter Fourteen:

Vigilance and Perseverance

Writing about protocols and remedies is far different than one-on-one counseling. When someone is sitting in front of me, I can see potential roadblocks based on the problems they've shared. My parting comments to every client are different, based on who they are and what their experiences have been. I don't know your specific story, but it is my hope that the parting words in these last chapters will inspire you and give you guidelines in identifying some potential pitfalls, as you engage in this challenging and proactive battle for freedom.

TWO REASONS PEOPLE FAIL

When it comes to implementing principles such as these, there are at least two reasons why people fail: our perception of happiness and our lack of vigilance.

OUR PERCEPTION OF HAPPINESS

We all have different ideas of happiness. C. S. Lewis explained it this way:

> *It would seem that Our Lord finds our desires not too strong, but too weak. We are half-hearted creatures, fooling about with drink and sex and ambition when infinite joy is offered us, like an ignorant*

child who wants to go on making mud pies in a slum because he cannot imagine what is meant by the offer of a holiday at the sea. We are far too easily pleased.[76]

Why do we settle for mud pies when we could be making sand castles at the beach? It is not that we want to believe the lies of the enemy or that we enjoy living in chaos, confusion, and conflict. It is because the perceived happiness we have now is known, and the happiness that God promises is unknown and not within our experience set.

As we wrestle with lies and truth, fear often takes root and will sound like this:[77] *You will be humiliated,* or *You will lose control,* or *Trusting God is irrational.* The enemy uses fear to keep us busy making mud pies. Why should we take a risk and reach out for everything God has planned for us? Moving from the known to the unknown can be daunting if we do not trust the One asking us to follow Him. We often choose to trust the enemy who has lied to us instead of the One who has always told the truth, who has always been faithful, and who will always make good on His promises. By staying bound to the familiar, we have no idea of the potential our life has in the hands of God. But by looking to God and believing He can and will do what He says, our lives and relationships can be forever changed. We can have a new track record of experiences that will help us through the next step into the unknown with God.

76. C. S. Lewis, *The Weight of Glory and Other Addresses* (New York: Macmillan Co., 1949).

77. If I see a 747 jet only a few hundred feet above the ground headed toward my house, I might just run in fear. That fear is real and does not involve lies. I believe this type of event accounts for only about 2 percent of our fears. The other 98 percent are fears based on lies of the enemy. Ask God for discernment to know the difference.

Every time we change our minds to be in harmony with God's thoughts and trust Him with each new unknown, we experience His faithfulness. He will then call us up to the next level, having built in us a confidence that can trust Him even more. This is not blind trust but the intricate, beautiful work of a lifetime. The crucifixion of Christ shows us that when Jesus hung on the cross feeling abandoned by almost everyone, even God, He said:

> *"Eli, Eli, lema sabachthani? (which means 'My God, my God, <u>why have you forsaken me?'</u>)" (Matt. 27:46; emphasis mine).*

He could have called it all off for His own benefit. Instead, in those horrible hours, He trusted His Father completely and did what was best for us. If He would do what was best for us under those terrible circumstances, why would He not do what is best for us now? What will it take for us to finally trust God? How many times will it take to believe that He will do what is best for us in every circumstance and always keep His promises?

We are not too different from the Israelites. They wandered in the wilderness for forty years because they distrusted God. If we focus on the known, fearing the unknown each time God presents us with truth, we will fail to trust Him, and the enemy's footprints will be all over our lives. If we focus on those past unknowns that surprised and thrilled us when we trusted God, and follow Him day by day, we can look at our present circumstance in a new and unimaginable level of existence with God in truth.

LACK OF VIGILANCE

With every new concept we set out to implement in our lives, it takes vigilance and perseverance for it to have a lasting effect.

In the parable of the sower in Matthew 13:1-23, Jesus describes four kinds of people who are shown His truth. In each circumstance, God is sowing seed into the heart, the heart represented by types of soil:

1. The heart described as the *path* is the hard heart that does not understand the truth. The enemy is there to snatch away the seed as soon as possible. The truth does not affect their life.

2. The heart described as the *rocky ground* is the heart that receives the truth with joy but has no root. When trouble comes, they forget what they learned, and their attention is drawn away from that truth they once received with joy.

3. The heart described as the *thorns* is the heart that "hears the word and understands it." However, their current problems, the worries of this life and the deceitfulness of wealth, choke out the truth they once received with joy.

4. The heart described as the *good soil* is the heart that hears and understands the truth and produces fruit. They trust God, follow and listen to the Holy Spirit when He speaks, and believe and embrace the truth He reveals to them.

Our job as we move forward is to be vigilant and to persevere by living a life that is completely devoted to the truth wherever it may show up. A life lived like this is never boring, but one adventure after another.

GOD'S COUNSEL REGARDING VIGILANCE AND PERSEVERANCE

"Since you have kept my command to endure patiently, I will also keep you from the hour of trial that is going to come on the whole world to test the inhabitants of the earth" (Rev. 3:10).

Submit yourselves, then, to God. Resist the devil, and he will flee from you (James 4:7).

Blessed is the one who perseveres under trial because, having stood the test, that person will receive the crown of life that the Lord has promised to those who love him (James 1:12).

Trust in the LORD with all your heart and lean not on your own understanding; in all your ways submit to him, and he will make your paths straight (Prov. 3:5-6).

Put on the full armor of God, so that you can take your stand against the devil's schemes (Eph. 6:11).

We want each of you to show this same diligence to the very end, so that what you hope for may be fully realized (Heb. 6:11).

You need to persevere so that when you have done the will of God, you will receive what he has promised (Heb. 10:36).

Consider it pure joy, my brothers and sisters, whenever you face trials of many kinds, because you know that the testing of your faith produces perseverance. Let perseverance finish its work so that you may be mature and complete, not lacking anything (James 1:2-4).

Being strengthened with all power according to his glorious might so that you may have great endurance and patience (Col. 1:11).

Be joyful in hope, patient in affliction, faithful in prayer (Rom. 12:12).

No temptation has overtaken you except what is common to mankind. And God is faithful; he will not let you be tempted beyond what you can bear. But when you are tempted, he will also provide a way out so that you can endure it (I Cor. 10:13).

I can do all this through him who gives me strength (Phi. 4:13).

May the God who gives endurance and encouragement give you the same attitude of mind toward each other that Christ Jesus had (Rom. 15:5).

But whoever looks intently into the perfect law that gives freedom, and continues in it—not forgetting what they have heard, but doing it—they will be blessed in what they do (James 1:25).

May the God of hope fill you with all joy and peace as you trust in him, so that you may overflow with hope by the power of the Holy Spirit (Rom. 15:13).

"Fixing our eyes on Jesus, the pioneer and perfecter of faith. For the joy set before him he endured the cross, scorning its shame, and sat down at the right hand of the throne of God (Heb. 12:2).

ADOPT A SPIRIT OF THANKFULNESS

When people complete their work on bitterness, I always ask them this question: "You would like Jesus to take these papers and burn them, right?" They always say, "Yes." Then I tell them, "Jesus will not take these away from you. Any issue you deal with must be given to Him voluntarily. He is always there with you, but it is your decision to make. Should you be tempted again, you must, again, decide between returning to your former bitterness or staying free.

Cast <u>all</u> your anxiety on him because he cares for you (I Pet. 5:7; emphasis mine).

The act of casting our worries and cares on Him is voluntary. God does not force us to do anything. Many remain in bondage because they are waiting for God to take their problems away from them.

With respect to bitterness, remember that forgiveness is a decision. We'd do well to live life as if we're surrounded by a bubble of a forgiving spirit, and anyone who bumps into that bubble gets forgiven. It is wise to intentionally decide to never be offended. Live in an atmosphere of forgiveness and remember that Jesus has freely forgiven us. We are now, undeservedly, set free.

We would do well to add thankfulness to our thoughts. This is an excellent way to maintain our freedom. Instead of listening to the enemy when he reminds us of the reasons we have for being bitter, thank God that we are free. Each morning offer up a prayer of thanksgiving and praise to God for your freedom and for His love. Thankfulness is a mighty weapon against the enemy and an excellent way to keep him out of our lives. The enemy hates our praises and thanks to God and doubtless does not want to hang around when we are doing so.

RIGOROUSLY CLING TO TRUTH

There are two aspects we need to consider when it comes to choosing truth over the enemy's lies. First, it takes courage to renounce the lies and believe and embrace the truth. This is no small task. This simple activity cuts directly across the desires and demands of our sinful nature. Here is what scripture says:

> *The person without the Spirit does not accept the things that come from the Spirit of God but considers them foolishness, and cannot understand them because they are discerned only through the Spirit (I Cor. 2:14).*

> *For the message of the cross is foolishness to those who are perishing, but to us who are being saved it is the power of God (I Cor. 1:18).*

Clinging to truth is not a task that can be done by the sinful, natural man (or "the flesh" as Paul refers to it). Discernment to discover lies and truth is not inherent to our sinful natures, but comes from the Holy Spirit who is at the center of any progress we make.

The mind governed by the flesh is death, but the mind governed by the Spirit is life and peace. The mind governed by the flesh is hostile to God; it does not submit to God's law, nor can it do so. Those who are in the realm of the flesh cannot please God (Rom. 8:6-8).

As we work through the lies we have believed for years, we will discern that we are regularly receiving wisdom from God regarding those lies. This discernment will encourage and give us confidence that the Holy Spirit lives in us, that we are under God's care as we move forward, and that He is helping us grow and become a complete and mature child of God.

For those who are led by the Spirit of God are the children of God. The Spirit you received does not make you slaves, so that you live in fear again; rather, the Spirit you received brought about your adoption to sonship. And by him we cry, "Abba, Father." The Spirit himself testifies with our spirit that we are God's children (Rom. 8:14-16).

Second, there is the courage needed to go where the truth leads us. There are times when we choose the lies of the enemy because we perceive the truth to be too costly. You may hear lies like *You can't do this, You will be humiliated if you go there, This goes against everything you have believed your whole life, Your friends and colleagues will say you are deceived,* or *Your spouse will leave you if they find out what you believe.*

It can be a joyful, enlightening experience to follow truth to its ultimate conclusion. Other times it can be frightening to consider the cost. To live a life completely committed to truth is not easy. The choice is not just about a lie we periodically renounce in favor of the truth but is a decision to embrace a lifestyle which demands that we always follow the truth wherever it requires us to go. It's a conscious change of our minds and hearts that will see us through those frightening times. At each step of our journey with God, we learn to trust Him; and with each additional step, we choose to trust Him <u>again</u> because of our previous experiences. In the end we will arrive at the victorious place truth has led us. Be courageous when it comes to embracing the truth. Let God lead you. You will not be disappointed in the end.

WE ARE NOT MAKING COOKIES

The freedom protocol cannot be approached as if following a recipe—life is more complex. At every turn, there are new opportunities to trust God and discover ever more beautiful things about Him and what He has planned for us to make us whole. As we move closer to God, what has worked for us in the past, may not work the same in a month or year later. A life of walking with God is a life that is fresh and new at every step. New challenges require new solutions previously not known or experienced. We have His promise that if we simply trust Him, He will show the way and see us through to victory.

"Do not fear or be dismayed because of this great multitude, for the battle is not yours but God's" (II Chron. 20:15b NASB).

But thanks be to God, who always leads us in triumph in Christ, and manifests through us the sweet aroma of the knowledge of Him in every place (II Cor. 2:14 NASB).

But we have this treasure in earthen vessels, so that the surpassing greatness of the power will be of God and not from ourselves; we are afflicted in every way, but not crushed; perplexed, but not despairing; persecuted, but not forsaken; struck down, but not destroyed;

always carrying about in the body the dying of Jesus, so that the life of Jesus also may be manifested in our body (II Cor. 4:7-10 NASB).

There is nothing that can come into your life today that you and God cannot handle together. Remember that on this journey, you are never alone.

I can do all this through him who gives me strength (Phil. 4:13).

Chapter Fifteen:

Is Jesus Necessary?

People have asked this question: Since it is the truth, and the truth about anything, that sets us free, is faith in Jesus a necessary factor to becoming free? Let's examine this question.

We only have a few details about the origin of sin. It appears to have started as the enemy, Satan, began to cherish lies in his heart about his identity and position.

> *"Your heart was lifted up because of your beauty; you corrupted your wisdom for the sake of your splendor . . ." (Ezek. 28:17a NKJV).*

As a result, Satan was cast out of heaven.

> *"How you are fallen from heaven, O Day Star, son of Dawn! How you are cut down to the ground, you who laid the nations low! You said in your heart, I will ascend to heaven; above the stars of God I will set my throne on high; I will sit on the mount of assembly in the far reaches of the north; I will ascend above the heights of the clouds; I will make myself like the Most High" (Isa. 14:12-15 ESV).*

This created being became so self-possessed and filled with pride, so enamored by his beauty and power, that he thought he could usurp the throne of an all-powerful God. It must be that because God rules His kingdom in such a loving, tender way, Satan must have viewed His ruling style as a weakness.

Genesis records Satan as being responsible for deceiving Adam and Eve into surrendering their lives and their dominion to him. They did this by believing his lies. Adam and Eve, who were once perfect, happy, and innocent, became sinful, naked, and full of shame as they stood before their creator. This is the life the enemy of our souls offers us in exchange for the abundant life God offers.

When Adam and Eve sinned, God, who is perfectly just and perfectly merciful, had a serious problem on His hands. He told them:

"But you must not eat from the tree of the knowledge of good and evil, for when you eat from it you will certainly die" (Gen. 2:17).

God could have stood in front of Adam and Eve in their guilt and nakedness and executed justice, leaving them as a little pile of ashes on the ground. That would have been justice but not mercy. Had this happened, the universe looking on would thereafter be serving God out of fear. Justice without mercy makes love impossible.

God also could have put His arms around Adam and Eve and said, "I know you didn't mean to do this, so I am going to give you another chance. Just don't do this again." That would have been mercy but not justice. Had this happened, the universe looking on would not take God and His commands seriously. Mercy without justice also makes love impossible.

At that moment, God's perfect nature of justice and mercy were in conflict. From a human perspective, this appears to be an impossible situation. However, there was a divine solution to this situation. The solution would require a very severe penalty—death. How can this penalty be paid and at the same time make it possible for God to be perfectly merciful? The answer is the cross of Christ.

At the cross, God not only punished sin in its entirety, but He took that punishment upon Himself.

All this is from God, who reconciled us to Himself through Christ . . . God was reconciling the world to Himself in Christ, not counting men's trespasses against them (II Corinthians 5:18-19 Berean Study Bible, BSB).

It is astounding that God stepped forward and personally took upon Himself the punishment of death that justice demanded. What kind of king would pass such a severe judgment on His creation and then step forward and take that very punishment upon Himself? This King could only be described as loving and compassionate, one who will *always* do what is best for His subjects, even at His own expense.

When God's commitment to our freedom is *not* understood, confusion about who He is will result. We may believe that we have gone too far to be forgiven, that God is unjust and really doesn't love us, or that He is an exacting, all-powerful being in the sky whose rules were made to make our lives miserable. The moment we believe these lies, we will misunderstand His actions. We should not allow our hearts to be ruled by our pain. And we should never allow the continuous stream of the enemy's lies to eclipse God's character of love and compassion toward us. God is not trying to keep you out of His kingdom. God is so committed to our freedom that He will at times let sin run its course so we can see the full nature of sin and its consequences, in hopes that we will flee from its bondage and desire the true freedom He wants to give us.

When God speaks truth into our lives, it is always an act of love. As we embrace it, our hearts are immediately filled with the fruit of the Spirit as described by Paul in Galatians chapter five. God is tenderly inviting each heart to embrace His loving, just, and merciful truth. It may be difficult to believe the truth when it forces us to look into our hearts and face the depths of sin to which we have fallen, but if you are dying of a disease and there is a cure, wouldn't you want to know the truth and the cure? Or would you want everyone to lie to you and tell you nothing is wrong?

THE DESIRE OF GOD

The enemy of our souls wants us to believe that God is forcing us to love Him and that He is unjust and unloving in all His ways. Yet, from the beginning, God's desire for mankind was that they would be free to love Him voluntarily. For love to be freely given requires a choice. Without the freedom to choose and even disappoint God, love cannot exist. Therefore, He did not force us to love Him or create us so we couldn't help but love Him. Love, to be real and meaningful, requires the giver to be free to love voluntarily.

As you implement the truths of God's design to rule over sin, you will gradually and naturally begin to enjoy freedom and peace. I have been told by many, who are not believers in Jesus Christ, that even simple truths, once believed and embraced, dispel chaos, confusion, and conflict.

God could refuse to give us any freedom until after we receive His Son but He doesn't do that. God in His love and mercy lets us taste freedom when we embrace even the common and self-evident truths that align with His ways. Do you want only a taste or the most you can get? For example, on an extremely hot day, would you rather have a sip of cool, refreshing water, or would you rather jump into the lake and be completely immersed in that cool, refreshing water? Why settle for a taste when you can have so much more.

In the late nineteenth and early twentieth centuries, donkeys were used in the Arizona silver mines. They were born, and lived and died, in the mines, never having seen the light of day. It was reported that if a donkey ever got out and saw daylight, they would never willingly go back into the mine again. If they were returned to the mine, they were constantly trying to get back to freedom. Freedom is infectious. Once you have tasted it, even the slightest bit, you always want more. When you experience that freedom, you have touched the heart of God. You will want to remain free and not to return to bondage.

GOD IS TRUTH IN EVERY SENSE

The apostle John tells us that Jesus became flesh to bring us the truth:

> *The Word [Jesus] became flesh and made his dwelling among us. We have seen his glory, the glory of the one and only Son, who came from the Father, full of grace and truth (John 1:14).*

This same Jesus, who is God and full of grace and truth, said:

> *"I am the way and the truth and the life. No one comes to the Father except through me" (John 14:6).*

This is not a self-centered statement of "my way or the highway." What this means is that Jesus is the only One who was capable of paying the infinite penalty of death for every person who has ever lived or will live on the earth. He is the One who, by His death, makes it possible for us to receive God's mercy and grace, which is joyfully given to us by God. Everything about Him is truth. Truth resides in Him and the truth that flows from Him brings peace, joy, and love. I'm not referring to doctrine, I'm referring to the heart of God and Jesus Christ. The lies that bring chaos, confusion, and conflict flow from the enemy of our souls. The battle is raging and although it is not often seen by us, it is a real battle between truth and falsehood.

Since it is the truth that sets you free, you have a choice as to the amount and quality of the truth you will believe and embrace. If you are courageous and want more than just a taste of the freedom God has in store for you, the answer to the title question of this chapter is YES. Jesus is the source and embodiment of truth. The decision is yours: settle for a taste of freedom, or dive in and immerse yourself in the truth to start that journey with Jesus right now. Jesus not only said that the truth will set you free, He said:

"So if the Son sets you free, you will be free indeed" (John 8:36).

You're invited to live a life full of peace, joy, and freedom by embracing and believing in Jesus Christ who is the way, the *truth*, and the life.

"I have come that they may have life, and have it to the full" (John 10:10b).

But the fruit of the Spirit is love, joy, peace, forbearance, kindness, goodness, faithfulness, gentleness, and self-control (Gal. 5:22-23a).

If you have not yet responded to the tender pleadings of the Savior, let me urge you to begin your journey with Him today. Jesus, Himself, will give you the abundant life full of hope and joy. No matter where you have come from, what you may have done, or how you have been wounded, embrace and believe in Him, the one who is the Truth—and believe the enemy's lies no longer.

If you want to receive Jesus now, you can pray a prayer similar to the following:

Dear Lord,

I am tired of the chaos and confusion in my life. I have believed Satan's lies far too long and they have led me into a life of bondage to sin. I believe in You, Jesus, and embrace You as my Savior.

Thank You for dying for me, saving me, and cleansing me from all my sin. Thank You for the remedies You have given me to be free. I ask You, Jesus, to stand at the door of my heart and protect me from the enemy's temptations and lies. I ask You to reveal any lies I still believe that mischaracterize You and the truth of Your plan for my life. Help me replace the lies in my heart with the truth, and help me to become one who will correctly represent Your character to others. Thank you, Jesus, for the new life You have given me and for the abundant life You have in store for me. Amen.

Lastly

TELL US YOUR EXPERIENCES

This book was written for your success. The freedom protocol may be applied to the issues you find to be problematic in your life, including but not limited to bitterness, immorality, pride, hypocrisy, addictions, anger, profanity, rebellion, low self-esteem, impatience, and greed. We would love to know how you are doing as you implement the freedom protocol, and we welcome feedback on how we can make this book more effective for you and others.

Visit our forum at https://www.h4hm.org. As you share, be courteous with those who are struggling. We look forward to hearing about your experiences. You can also email us at info@h4hm.org. As we share experiences, we are confident you will discover that the freedom protocol and remedies God has provided will be applicable to other issues in your life we have not covered here.

To purchase *You're Invited* in singles or bulk, visit the Healing For The Heart Ministries Bookstore at https://h4hm.org/bookstore.

May the Lord bless you in this new and exciting adventure of your life.

Acknowledgements

There are several people who have played an important part in getting this book written and published that I wish to thank:

- Cissa Saladino, my wife, who has been incredibly supportive and consistently urged me to "write the book." Without her this book would never have been written.

- Joseph Cole Taylor, my nineteen-year-old grandson, who asked some of the most profound questions and made many astute observations about the book. He encouraged me by showing that the young can understand these protocols and remedies and by immediately putting these protocols to work in his own life.

- Bridget Saladino and Amanda Taylor, my daughters; and Sean Taylor, my son-in-law, who patiently listened to me explain these protocols and engaged in discussion with me to challenge my thinking.

- John Regier, director and founder of Caring for the Heart Ministries, who first put me on to the ideas that sin is the way we grant the enemy ground (jurisdiction) in our lives, that these strongholds can be broken, and this ground (jurisdiction) can be given back to God.

- Gary Martel, a good friend, who spent hours with me discussing the freedom protocol and patiently challenged me to explain myself more clearly. His successfully making use of the freedom protocol, years after we spoke, has been a real source of encouragement to me.

- Dale Lowell, a dear friend, the first person to read the manuscript, encouraged me with his excitement about the book. His comments, insights, and recommendations are seen throughout this book.

- Pastor Troy Haagenson, whose attention to detail and theological acumen have kept me on track and improved the readability of this book.

- Jerry Willis, a friend from college, who took on the review of this book with an incredible tenacity. He was bold and not afraid to tell me what he thought, challenging my expression of ideas. Jerry has a way of reducing fifteen words to five. Conversations with him helped me make important parts of this book much clearer.

- Jere Webb, a dear friend and skilled theologian, who was not afraid to boldly tell me what he thought and to challenge my ideas. His encouragement will never be forgotten.

- Ed and Cindy Schultz, very dear friends, who were among the first to encourage me to "write the book."

- Brian Stevens, a good friend, who along with others urged me to write this book when I was thinking of writing something else. He showed me the importance of this work.

- Cheri Peters, a good friend and an outstanding author, who encouraged me to write this book because "people need this information." Thank you, Cheri, for lighting a fire under me to get this book written.

- Terry Chesnut, a good friend, who took the time to look at each line in the book and give me valuable feedback to challenge my ideas. He does not miss much.

- Many others like Frank Brannon, Tim Gross, Stan Nelson, David Ruskjer, and Sara Baer, who challenged these protocols and helped me discover better ways to communicate to the reader.

- My Bible study class, who studied this book for over fourteen weeks. They were a huge influence in helping me discover ways to adjust the book to accommodate a weekly Bible study.

- Todd and Mindy Hubbard, and Tammy Molfino, who deserve the medal of honor for putting up with the me during the entire publishing process. Their superb editing skills are evident throughout this book.

Printed in the USA
CPSIA information can be obtained
at www.ICGtesting.com
JSHW021912120524
62807JS00004B/131